THE GUIDE TO

ASTROLOGY

NOVEMBER
OCTOBER
SEPTEMBER
MARTIVS
MAIVS

THE GUIDE TO ASTROLOGY

Understanding the secrets of the stars and planets

LORI REID

Parragon

Bath · New York · Singapore · Hong Kong · Cologne · Delhi · Melbourne

First published by Parragon in 2008

Parragon
Queen Street House
4 Queen Street
Bath BA1 1HE, UK

ISBN: 978-1-4075-1130-6

Printed in China

Created and produced for Parragon by
Blue Island Publishing Limited.

CONTENTS

THE BASICS OF ASTROLOGY

Astrology is the study of cosmic influence on our lives. The position of the Sun, Moon, Planets, and Stars at the time of your birth shapes your character, fortunes, and relationships with other people throughout your whole life. In this section, we introduce the 12 signs of the Zodiac and explain how they relate to the Planets, Houses, and Aspects on a birth chart to form a profile of a subject's personality, life, and future prospects.

A computer-generated image of the Sun with Mercury, Venus, Earth, Mars, Jupiter, and Saturn in a line

THE ZODIAC SIGNS

Astrology is a rich and fascinating insight into the interconnectedness of all things. In the signs of the Zodiac we find a microcosm of the universe—parallels between what we see in the cosmos and all earthly matters, both animate and inanimate.

WHAT IS THE ZODIAC?

The word Zodiac comes from the Greek for "ring of animals." It refers to the pathway along which the planets orbit in the heavens. This circular band is technically called the ecliptic and is divided into 12 sections known as the astrological signs. Most of the signs are named after animals, such as the lion, crab, goat (hence, Zodiac).

Ptolemy, the most influential astrologer in Ancient Greece

You probably already know which sign of the Zodiac you belong to. The page opposite shows them all in order beginning with Aries. Belonging to a sign means that you were born during the period when the Sun was traveling through that sign. In fact, you may sometimes hear the signs of the Zodiac being referred to as Sun signs. Essentially, the signs are markers for roughly locating when in the year people are born. Saying you're a Sagittarian, for example, tells us that the Sun was in the sign of the Archer, and that you celebrate your birthday between the last week of November and the first three weeks of December.

Map of planetary orbits by Tycho Brahe, a 16th-century astrologer

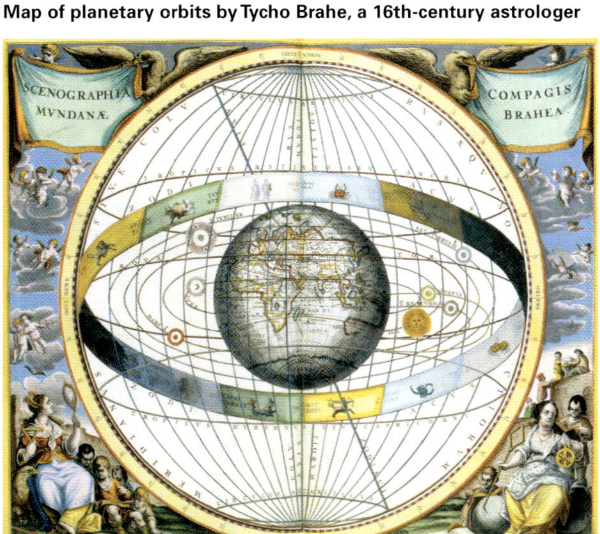

SIGNIFICANCE OF THE SIGNS

The 12 signs of the Zodiac are the foremost part of a system that highlights the similarities between groups of people and helps us to understand and predict human behaviors, circumstances, and events. This system is based on an ancient body of knowledge about the cosmos and the significance of the exact location of stars and planets at the moment of a person's birth.

The signs have a complex layering of associations and groupings. For example, signs that show resistance to change are classified as "Fixed." Signs associated with chatty, intellectual people are assigned to the "Air" element. The properties of certain minerals, plants, and other earthly matters are associated with particular planets. More details about these associations are on the following pages and in the Signs section.

Your sign says a lot about you. Simply saying you're a Leo or a Taurus or a Scorpio is actually a shorthand way of describing what type of person you are, what you like and dislike, and what you aim for and hope for in life.

INTRODUCING THE SIGNS

♈ **1. ARIES** **March 21–April 20**

Aries is symbolized by the horns of the Ram and represents the time of spring when the land is greening and the sap is rising. People of this sign are assertive, impatient, open, and direct. *See pages 24–29*

♉ **2. TAURUS** **April 21–May 21**

Steady, practical, and creative, Taurus is the builder of the Zodiac. Associated with material goods and earthly pleasures, it is symbolized by the head and horns of the Bull. *See pages 30–35*

♊ **3. GEMINI** **May 22–June 22**

First of the human creatures and symbolized by the Twins, Gemini represents communication. Talkative, curious, and restless, this is a busy sign, perpetually in motion. *See pages 36–41*

♋ **4. CANCER** **June 23–July 23**

Symbol of home, family, and hearth, Cancer is the sign of caring and nurturing. Parenthood and conservation are deeply entwined, represented by the protective shell of the Crab. *See pages 42–47*

♌ **5. LEO** **July 24–August 23**

Symbolized by the Lion, king of the beasts, Leo is the sign of nobility. Proud and arrogant, yet loyal and brave, this sign is ablaze with warmth and the well-being of summer. *See pages 48–53*

♍ **6. VIRGO** **August 24–September 23**

Organization, duty, routine, and service come under the dominion of this sign. Ruled by the Maiden carrying a sheaf of corn, Virgo represents work and health. *See pages 54–59*

♎ **7. LIBRA** **September 24–October 23**

Marking the halfway point in the year, Libra is aptly symbolized by the Scales because it deals with balance and equilibrium. Relationships, sociability, and harmony are its aims. *See pages 60–65*

♏ **8. SCORPIO** **October 24–November 22**

The Scorpion will lash out with its deadly sting if provoked. This is an intense sign that is associated with privacy and secrecy. Sex, power, and regeneration are the deeper issues. *See pages 66–71*

♐ **9. SAGITTARIUS** **November 23–December 21**

Expansive, freedom-loving, and philosophical, Sagittarius is the sign of travel. The Archer reaches for distant places and far-reaching intellectual concepts. *See pages 72–77*

♑ **10. CAPRICORN** **December 22–January 20**

Capricorn is the sign of authority: ambitious, conservative, and achievement-motivated. Symbolizing the profile of the Goat's face and side horn, it represents the social climber. *See pages 78–83*

♒ **11. AQUARIUS** **January 21–February 19**

This is a sign associated with sociability, teamwork, and group events. Aquarius sweeps away the past and looks to the future with its friendly, inventive, and thoroughly progressive nature. *See pages 84–89*

♓ **12. PISCES** **February 20–March 20**

Dreamy, sensitive, imaginative, and receptive traits are characteristic of Pisces. The symbol of two fish tied together but swimming in opposite directions brings the cycle of the Zodiac to an end. *See pages 90–95*

SIGN GROUPINGS

Historically, the signs of the Zodiac have been classified into specific groups that help to give further information about how they work. The most important groupings are Yin-Yang, Elements, and Qualities.

Taurus may be a Bull but it is also classed as a Yin, or feminine, sign

YIN-YANG

A term borrowed from Chinese philosophy, Yin-Yang is a distinction to the signs, which are deemed negative or positive, or else feminine or masculine *(see box)*. The even-numbered signs are considered Yin, negative, and feminine. Members of these signs tend to be shyer individuals, preferring to follow rather than take the lead. The Yang, positive, and masculine signs are the odd-numbered ones. People belonging to the Yang signs tend, on the whole, to be more assertive and self-expressive.

THE ELEMENTS

Each sign is ruled by one of the four Elements – Earth, Air, Fire, and Water *(see box)*. The Elements add extra depth to the understanding and appreciation of the signs. And because certain Elements have an affinity to one another, this information is very useful when working with issues concerning partnerships and compatibility.

THE QUALITIES

While the Elements classify the signs according to temperament, the Qualities (which are also known as quadruplicities), group the signs according to how each uses its energy and takes action on a day-to-day basis. There are three categories of Qualities—Cardinal, Fixed, and Mutable—each of which contains four signs *(see box)*.

ESSENTIAL GROUPINGS AT A GLANCE

YIN-YANG	
Yin	Taurus, Cancer, Virgo, Scorpio, Capricorn, Pisces *negative, feminine, internalizing*
Yang	Aries, Gemini, Leo, Libra, Sagittarius, Aquarius *positive, masculine, assertive*
THE ELEMENTS	
Earth	Taurus, Virgo, Capricorn *down-to-earth, practical, industrious*
Air	Gemini, Libra, Aquarius *clever, social, verbally expressive*
Fire	Aries, Leo, Sagittarius *bright, active, enthusiastic, impulsive*
Water	Cancer, Scorpio, Pisces *sensitive, compassionate, emotionally-driven*
THE QUALITIES	
Cardinal	Aries, Cancer, Libra, Capricorn *assertive, good leader, likes change*
Fixed	Taurus, Leo, Scorpio, Aquarius *determined, persistent, likes the status quo*
Mutable	Gemini, Virgo, Sagittarius, Pisces *flexible, adaptable, cooperative, a go-between*

Fire, one of the essential four Elements in astrology, is associated with Aries, Leo, and Sagittarius

A table of the signs used by apothecaries in the Middle Ages, showing how different parts of the body relate to the 12 signs of the Zodiac

SIGN AFFINITIES

As well as the essential groupings, each sign has numerous affinities with other things in the cosmos and on Earth. Most importantly, each sign has a ruling planet. *(For more on the planets, see pages 14–19.)* Other examples include minerals, colors, plants, and places linked with the Zodiac. The origins of many such associations have been lost in the mists of time. Others come from studies undertaken by modern astrologers.

THE BODY & HEALING PLANTS

In ancient times, knowledge of astrology was instrumental in the understanding and treating of disease. Physicians studied the nature and properties of ill-health according to the planetary influences. Each part of the body and each organic function was seen to correspond with a particular planet or sign of the Zodiac. Saturn, for instance, was said to rule the bones, and so by inference, Capricorn was assigned governance over the skeleton.

By the Middle Ages, physicians had a vast knowledge of the medicinal effects of flowers, herbs, and plants at their disposal. Each plant, either because of its properties or its specific curative powers, was ascribed to the dominion of one or other of the planets. Thus, by matching the plant to the planet, and the planet to the disease, it was possible for the physician to effect a cure. For example, feverfew was attributed to the rulership of Venus, goddess of love. Appropriately, this herb was used to ease gynecological problems. *Matricaria*, the plant's Latin name, further alludes to its properties and application. Garlic, on the other hand, was associated with Mars because the bulb possesses "vehement heat"—heat being a Martian characteristic. Lavender, ruled by Mercury—planet of the mind—was used to cure "pains of the head and brain" or taken to prevent dizziness. Dandelion, governed by Jupiter, the ruler of Sagittarius, was invaluable to physicians as a cleanser for the liver.

OTHER ASSOCIATIONS

As with the healing plants, the origin of many other associations come from affinities with the ruling planets. For example, red is the color assigned to Aries because Aries is ruled by Mars, the red planet. The metal quicksilver, also known as mercury, is associated with Gemini because Gemini's ruling planet is Mercury. By extension, certain gemstones are linked to signs because of their color or healing properties. Days of the week are linked with the signs of the Zodiac through their ruling planets *(see page 18)*.

Less obviously, certain locations on Earth—cities, countries, and even entire continents—are linked with particular signs, because astrologers have found affinities between locations and the cosmos, from their history or geographical character. The country of Australia, for example, is linked with Sagittarius. This means not only that Australia has Sagittarian characteristics but also that it might be a country favorable to a Sagittarian person's interests.

THE BIRTH CHART

Literally meaning "a picture of the hour," your horoscope, or birth chart, is a diagram that represents the heavens at the moment you were born. How your personal chart looks—which signs line up with which houses, and the location of individual planets—depends on three key factors: your date, exact time, and geographical place of birth.

THE BASIC WHEEL

In astrology, a person's birth chart is drawn up in the shape of a wheel cut through by spokes to form 12 segments. Each segment is known as a "house," which describes a particular part of the skies and plots the Zodiacal sign and planets that were inhabiting that sector at the moment of your birth. The spokes, or dividers, are called cusps. Although the wheel itself and the arrangement of houses is similar, everyone's chart is different, which is a testimony to each person's individuality.

Manually plotting cosmic positions for a birth chart

Referring to the basic wheel shown below, think of the horoscope as a clock face. At 9 o'clock is your ascendant. This is the point in the sky that was coming into view on the eastern horizon at the moment of your birth. The sign, and any planets, that cover this area describe how you look to the outside world and the characteristics that a stranger would pick up on first meeting you. This is your outward persona—often quite different to the "real" you that is described by the sector in which the Sun is located.

THE HOROSCOPE WHEEL

This is the basic horoscope wheel. Each segment—numbered here for easy reference—is a house that contains an area of your affairs. When you create a birth chart, the positioning of signs and planets within the wheel determines the nature of that part of your life.

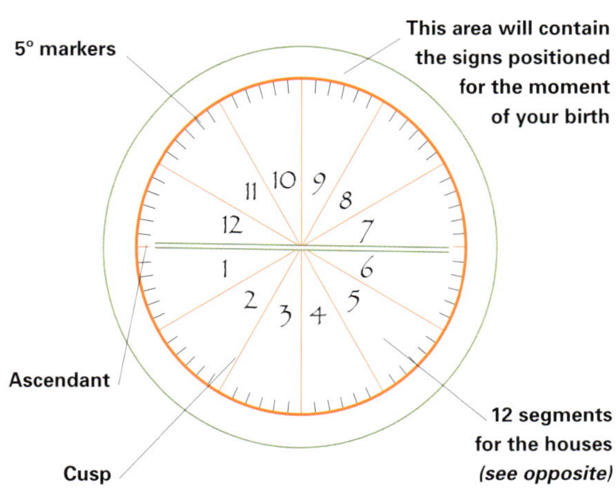

CREATING A BIRTH CHART

You can create a chart for yourself or anyone else if you know the exact time and location of birth. If you do not know the exact hour and minute, then use noon as a guide, although the chart will not be as accurate as it could be.

There are some good Web sites *(see page 96)* that can automatically calculate the cosmic positions for anyone's moment of birth over the last 100 years or so. This is the easiest way to have your natal chart created within seconds. Alternatively, you can consult published ephemeris tables to draw up a chart manually. Once you have the chart, you can see which planets and signs fall into the segments, or houses *(left)*. You can then use the guide to houses opposite as the starting point for interpreting your personal chart.

THE HOUSES ON THE BIRTH CHART

1 THE FIRST HOUSE

This house describes your basic personality; the picture you paint of yourself for the outside world to see; your physical appearance; your well-being. Any planets in this segment add extra detail to your looks and behavior.

2 THE SECOND HOUSE

This is the house governing material possessions. Here you will find information relating to your earnings and income, and your sense of personal security.

3 THE THIRD HOUSE

Communication is the key to this house. The sign and planets describe how you express yourself. They also reveal your relationship to siblings and neighbors, and to your immediate environment.

4 THE FOURTH HOUSE

The fourth house is all about your home and family. It reveals essentials of your childhood, blood-bonds, roots, and, importantly, your mother.

5 THE FIFTH HOUSE

Leisure, pleasure, children, creativity, and romance are the affairs described by this sector. The sign and planets here reveal your level of physical and mental fertility; your hobbies and spare time pursuits. It also highlights your luck and good fortune.

6 THE SIXTH HOUSE

Health, work, and well-being; day-to-day activities; hygiene and sanitation are shown here. Essentially, this house deals with the way we accept our responsibilities and carry out our duties.

7 THE SEVENTH HOUSE

The seventh house is the sector for partnerships and relationships, both intimate and professional. This part of your birth chart describes your marriage and/or your partners in life.

8 THE EIGHTH HOUSE

Serious and somber issues, such as mortgages, wills, legacies, and escrow, are dealt with here. So are the very deep issues of surgery and death. Sexual attitudes and preferences are also revealed by the sign and planets in this area.

9 THE NINTH HOUSE

This sector deals with education and higher learning, along with philosophy, religion, and law. Travel to distant places and faraway affairs are revealed by what is placed here.

10 THE TENTH HOUSE

Here is the midheaven of your chart, which deals with your worldly affairs: reputation, ambition, status, and career. Authority figures, your father, and your boss are described in this zone.

11 THE ELEVENTH HOUSE

Friends, associates, group affairs, and generally how you get along with other people are all the business of this sector. Your hopes and dreams are also highlighted here.

12 THE TWELFTH HOUSE

This house reveals our innermost fears, dreams, and secret fantasies. This is where we hide away from the world. It deals with seclusion, hospitals, prisons, and our own self-undoing.

THE PLANETS

The characteristics of the "planets"—a term that includes the Sun and Moon in astrology—have fascinated humans for centuries. They are focal points of energy, exerting powerful influences according to their position in the birth chart.

THE WANDERERS

In ancient times, the planets were known as the "wanderers" because, unlike the "Fixed" stars, they move through the heavens, changing positions on a day-to-day basis. For the sake of convenience, astrologers call the Sun and the Moon planets, although the former is technically a star, and the latter is a satellite of the Earth.

The planets travel at different speeds through the heavens, and each rules over a specific sign *(see page 17)*. Mercury and Venus each have rulership over 2 signs because there are only 10 planets for 12 signs of the Zodiac.

THE SUN'S JOURNEY THROUGH THE ZODIAC

As seen from Earth, each year the Sun passes through the 12 signs of the Zodiac, shown here as symbols.

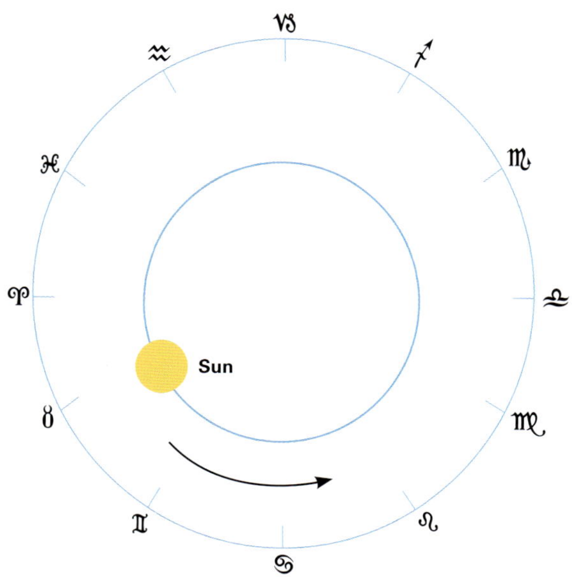

Medieval chart of the Sun and planets in relation to the Earth

THE SUN

Spending one month in each sign, the Sun takes a year to complete its cycle through the Zodiac. Astrologically, it is the "life battery" representing as it does your vitality, energy, and creative power.

At the moment of your birth the Sun immediately locates your position in the horoscope and by its placement describes your character, your spirit, and your power of will. It symbolizes your essence, your drive, motivation, and conscious self. How you express yourself, how you carry yourself, and how you launch yourself onto the world stage very much depends on the placement of the Sun in your chart at the moment you were born.

From this point, the Sun begins its journey around the 12 signs, returning, each year on your birthday, to the exact position it occupied at your birth. When the Sun returns to your sign, it re-energizes you, symbolically giving you a shot in

Illustration of the Sun and planets nearest to Earth

the arm and triggering a whole new 12-monthly cycle of experiences and events.

As it moves through each of the signs in the course of a year, the Sun will meet and pass each of the other planets as individually they, too, make their way around the Zodiac. Depending on the angles formed during these meetings—whether the two cross close by, find themselves at 90 degrees, or face each other in opposition across the chart—your life experiences on those occasions will be colored in either a harmonious or discordant way *(see also The Aspects, pages 20–21)*.

THE MOON

From new moon to first crescent, through full to gibbous, then last crescent and back to new again, it takes the Moon just under a month to move through its phases and complete its cycle around the Earth. It is this ever changing face, reflecting as it does the light of the Sun, that makes the Moon such an appropriate mirror for our own changing moods, feelings, and impressions.

Astrologically, the Moon is the natural ruler of Cancer and is associated with the element Water and with the tides on Earth. In our horoscopes, the Moon represents our emotions, and how we respond and instinctively react to people and situations. It also represents our imagination and intuitive processes. Associated with the Hunter goddess Diana, the Moon is the natural symbol of women and, more especially, of motherhood.

Unlike the Sun, which spends a month in each sign, the Moon is in each for little more than two days at a time, zipping around all 12 signs of the Zodiac in about 27 and a half days.

Mercury, messenger of the gods in ancient mythology

MERCURY

The closest planet to the Sun, Mercury takes just 88 days to orbit our solar star. Perhaps it is precisely because of its great speed that in Ancient Roman times Mercury became known as the messenger of the gods, rushing hither and thither to spread news and information.

In the birth chart, Mercury rules Gemini and Virgo, and represents the intellect. How we think, reason, and calculate, our desire to learn, our curiosity, and our need to know: these all form part of the mental activity that is ruled by this planet. All forms of communication, too, come under Mercury's jurisdiction—languages, schooling, and even the postal service. Three times a year the planet turns "retrograde" (an apparent slowing down of motion). It's during these times that we experience all sorts of delays and frustrations, when people change their mind, things get lost in the mail, new equipment will fail, or something else is bound to go wrong.

VENUS

Lying between Mercury and the Earth, Venus has rulership over two signs: Taurus and Libra. Although one is an Earth sign and the other belongs to the element Air, they do share a love of culture, creativity, and ease, which is directly attributable to the influence of Venus. For this is the planet of good things, of leisure and pleasure, of indulgence, beauty, and harmony. Above all, we know Venus as the goddess of love, and indeed wherever this planet is positioned in your birth chart will be where you express yourself most affectionately. Romance comes under Venus' sway, as do love affairs. Our artistic appreciation is also conditioned by this planet in our charts. Whether we have refined tastes or tend to go overboard on the accoutrements very much depends on where Venus is situated and the kind of contacts she makes with the other planets.

MARS

Smaller than Earth but farther from the Sun, Mars takes 687 days to orbit the Sun. Classically, Mars was the god of war, and astrologically this planet is associated with masculine drive and aggression. How appropriate then that it shimmers red in the night sky! Its influence in the chart is fiery, energetic, and assertive. In matters of the heart, Mars adds passion. To ambition it brings drive, and to physical energy it supplies stamina and strength. Mars is a dynamic force: impulsive, enthusiastic, and courageously bold. But beware. Get out of bed on the wrong side and Mars can make you impatient, quarrelsome, and downright rude!

Venus, the goddess of beauty, harmony, and love

THE PLANETS AT A GLANCE

		ORBIT	GOVERNANCE	SIGN RULERSHIP
☉	SUN	Earth orbits in 1 year	God of Light Planet of the Self	Leo
☽	MOON	27.3 days to orbit Earth	Goddess of Hunting Planet of the Emotions	Cancer
☿	MERCURY	88 Earth days	Messenger of the Gods Planet of Communication	Gemini and Virgo
♀	VENUS	225 Earth days	Goddess of Love Planet of Harmony	Taurus and Libra
♂	MARS	687 Earth days	God of War Planet of Energy	Aries (also Scorpio in ancient traditions)
♃	JUPITER	12 Earth years	King of the Gods Planet of Bounteousness	Sagittarius (also Pisces in ancient traditions)
♄	SATURN	30 Earth years	God of Time Planet of Discipline	Capricorn (also Aquarius in ancient traditions)
♅	URANUS	84 Earth years	God of the Heavens Planet of Rebellion	Aquarius
♆	NEPTUNE	165 Earth years	God of the Sea Planet of Illusion	Pisces
♇	PLUTO	249 Earth years	God of the Underworld Planet of Power	Scorpio

Jupiter as depicted in a painting in the Villa Medici in Florence

JUPITER

Larger than life and with an appetite to match, Jupiter is the giant planet of our solar system. Known as the "greater benefic," this is the guardian angel, the luck-bringer, the sugar daddy. Jupiter takes 12 years to orbit the Sun and spends roughly one year in each sign. Wherever Jupiter is located in our birth charts, it will amplify and expand those affairs. For example, you can expect opportunities galore when you're looking for a new job and this bounteous planet is visiting your 10th house of career. Converting a humble abode into a palace will be desirable when expansive Jupiter visits the "hearth and home" sector of your chart.

The flip-side to Jupiter is that it can be hard to control those risk-taking urges, to avoid embarrassing your friends with your foghorn laughter or to refrain from wearing quite so many clashing colors when Jupiter is in your sector of leisure and pleasure. Moreover, when this planet of indulgence and largesse hits your health zone, controlling your weight is an uphill struggle.

THE ANCIENT SEVEN

The seven "wanderers" that are visible to the naked eye—namely the Sun, Moon, and five planets nearest to Earth—have very ancient links with the seven-day week and seven metals. Modern-day astrologers remember these age-old associations even where the original connection has long been obscured in practice or even in language. The planets that were not discovered until after the invention of telescopes in the 17th century—namely Uranus, Neptune, and Pluto—are not included on this list. After the latter were discovered, many astrologers reclassified the ruling planets of three signs (Scorpio, Pisces, and Aquarius), but some of their associations with the ancient seven remain.

	Sacred Metal	Sacred Day
Sun	Gold	Sunday (English Sun's Day)
Moon	Silver	Monday (English Moon's Day)
Mercury	Mercury	Wednesday (French Mercredi)
Venus	Copper	Friday (Italian Venerdi)
Mars	Iron	Tuesday (French Mardi)
Jupiter	Tin	Thursday (Spanish Jueves)
Saturn	Lead	Saturday (English Saturn's Day)

SATURN

Famous task master of the universe, Saturn is the converse of Jupiter. Where Jupiter gives and expands, Saturn takes and contracts. This planet remains in each sign for about two and a half years, in which time it prunes and culls, limits, and restricts. Saturn teaches us discipline and responsibility. Try to cut corners, to be wanton and wasteful, and this planet will crack the whip. Learning to work within its guidelines, however—to order and systematize, to garner, and conserve—will earn you valuable life bonuses when this planet's around.

A view of Saturn, astrology's planet of self-discipline

URANUS

First discovered in 1781, Uranus is the planet of change, and represents rebellion and revolution. When this planet travels through a specific sector of your chart, batten down the hatches! Nothing it touches will be left as it was before. Taking an average human life span to orbit the Sun, Uranus stays in one sign on average for about seven years. In your birth chart, Uranus shows where your originality lies. As it moves through the houses, it sweeps away the old and brings in the new. When it lands in the fourth sector, for example, you might decide on a radical makeover for your home or even to move. In the seventh, it can bring a change of marital status, a wedding, or a divorce. When Uranus reaches your Ascendant *(see page 12)*, you can expect a remarkable personal transformation and a change of attitude to almost everything you felt before.

NEPTUNE

Planet of illusion, Neptune smudges boundaries and deconstructs reality. Discovered in 1846 by mathematical prediction rather than direct observation, this planet is named after the god of the sea, and its influence washes us off our feet. There is a nebulous, other-worldliness about Neptune's energy, on the one hand stirring up our imagination and producing wonderful creative visions in art, literature, and music. On the other hand, Neptune's insubstantiality clouds our judgment, and makes us evasive and vague.

Remaining in a sign for up to 14 years, Neptune is the planet of idealism and dreams. It is also the planet of escapism and self-delusion. Used positively, the energy of Neptune can help us to create wonderful things. Negatively, it can lead to deception, fantasy, addiction, and pretence.

PLUTO

The farthest known planet from the Sun, Pluto takes nearly 250 years to journey around the solar system, but such is its erratic orbit that it can remain in a sign from as little as 15 years to as long as 30. Although it is far away, Pluto is associated with cold power, steely conflict, and the fight for supremacy. This is an intense influence—deep, dark, and mysterious. Associated with regeneration, Pluto's influence concerns the elimination of all that is outworn in order to make space for regrowth and new life. Where it is placed in the birth chart shows which area of your affairs will come under constant redevelopment and renewal. Pluto is also the planet of psychoanalysis, paranormal forces, sex, and, ultimately, death.

Statue in Florence depicting Neptune, the Roman god of the sea, and water nymphs

THE ASPECTS

The aspects are significant angles formed between the planets as they travel around the Zodiac. On a birth chart they are shown as symbols in specific areas. Some enhance the influence of planets they relate to; others inhibit the influence.

ANGLES IN THE SKY

As the planets move through the heavens, each at its own speed, they will at various points pass each other, sometimes close by, sometimes as if coming around a corner or, at other times, find themselves facing each other on opposite sides of the Zodiac belt. These "meetings" are recorded as geometric angles, and the patterns that are formed are called "aspects."

The aspects are basically the relationship that any two planets form with one another at any point along their route. Aspects are important because they create an interplay of energy, combining and modifying the influences that are being given out by the planets concerned.

Consider for a moment a meeting between indulgent Venus and Jupiter, planet of plenty. If this takes place in your health zone, for example, you would probably find it impossible to refuse a cream cake or three. Replace Jupiter with stern Saturn here, and the situation is quite different. Not only will you resist the cream cakes with a will of iron, but you're also likely to take yourself off to the gym to pump iron for an hour or two in order to get yourself back into shape.

As with all experiences, some of these relationships are happy and comfortable while others can be gritty and difficult. It is the type of aspect, or angle that is formed, that tells us whether the energies given out are harmonious or discordant—traditionally referred to by astrologers as "soft" or "hard."

MAJOR ASPECTS		
☌	**Conjunction**	0°
⚹	**Sextile**	60°
□	**Square**	90°
△	**Trine**	120°
☍	**Opposition**	180°

There are five major aspects ranging from the conjunction at 0° to the opposition at 180°. In between are the sextile at 60°, the square at 90°, and the trine at 120°. Rather like shorthand, each aspect is depicted by a symbol on birth charts, as shown in the box.

CONJUNCTION

A conjunction occurs when two planets come together in close proximity (not necessarily on top of each other) and in your chart are placed in the same sign. Whether this aspect is hard or soft depends on the two planets involved. In general, however, conjunctions are considered powerful aspects since they blend, intensify, and amplify the energies of the combined pair.

SEXTILE

Here the planets are two signs apart and together form an acute angle of 60°. Generally, planets in sextile aspect are favorably disposed to one another. Because they enhance each other's qualities, this relationship has a harmonious effect and is therefore considered a soft aspect.

Diagram of conjunctions from a 17th-century celestial atlas

SQUARE

Situated three signs apart in the chart, a square aspect at 90° is considered tense. Here there is a sense of vying, a boxing match is taking place with each planet trying to get supremacy and together giving off a discordant energy. Because of the gritty, challenging feel to this aspect it is classified as hard.

TRINE

Planets in trine aspects are located four signs apart —120°—which places them in the same element. Thus, the energies of these two work through the same medium and reinforce each other. This aspect, then, is classed as soft, with planetary energies that are mutually helpful and supportive.

OPPOSITION

The opposition is a hard aspect. Here, two planets are facing each other across the chart and in a confrontational situation. These planets are in conflict, at odds with each other, pulling and pushing in different directions. When two planets are in opposition, a tug-of-war is taking place, and who wins very much depends on the strength of the characters involved.

YOU AND YOUR SIGN

The sign that the Sun was in at the time of your birth describes a lot about your character. In this section, we look at each of the 12 Sun signs in detail, and see how different areas of our lives are shaped by the signs. Included are the essential areas of childhood, career, relationships, and health. There is guidance to love pairings between the signs, and pointers to the best and worst traits of each. Also included are lists of symbols and associations, and examples of famous personalities for each of the 12 signs.

A 19th-century Zodiac clock in Prague, showing the symbols and allegorical pictures for each sign

♈ ARIES

Since ancient times, Aries has been considered to be the first sign of the Zodiac because it marks the beginning of Spring. Its symbol is the Ram of mythology, with curling horns. Aries people are highly dynamic, and they enjoy being first.

ARIES BASICS

Have you noticed how Aries people are always rushing here, there, and everywhere? This is hardly surprising when you consider that Aries not only belongs to the Fire element *(see page 10)* but is also classed as a Cardinal, or outgoing and ambitious sign. All this means that, just like a bush fire when it takes hold, Aries people are unstoppable in whatever they do.

The Ram is the symbol of Aries—strong, powerful, and leading the flock. In fact, Aries is never happier than when out in front. Taking a back seat, hanging around at the end of the line, or shuffling behind the dawdlers is, quite frankly, an Aries person's idea of hell. Heaven for this sign is all about being in the vanguard. Aries is one of life's pioneers. Not the most homely of people, nor the most domesticated, Aries is not seduced by soft living or sophisticated lifestyles. The mission in life is to push the boundaries. Physically or metaphorically, Aries courageously strikes out into virgin territory and, no matter how rough it gets, no-one can tough it out quite as well as an Aries.

Direct, outspoken, and decisive sums up this sign. An Aries person is a wonderfully spirited, feisty individual. A daredevil, driven by a passion for life and by a hunger for anything new, Aries puts 120 percent into everything. No wonder, then, that people feel compelled to follow the leadership of Aries.

ARIES

Place in Zodiac First
Birth Dates March 21–April 20
Symbol The Ram

WHAT MAKES ARIES HAPPY?

- Action movies
- Fast cars
- Acquiring the latest gadget on sale and showing it off to friends
- Computer games, electronic chess
- Exploring new places
- Survival gear and camping under the stars
- Wild parties
- Team games
- "Been there, done that, and got the T-shirt"—first!

YOUNG RAMS

The Aries youngster very definitely has a mind of his or her own. Children born under this sign tend to be willful souls, determined to do their own thing—how and when they want. They are probably the noisiest in the maternity ward and the first to crawl, so eager are they to explore their surroundings and take control of their world. The fearlessness that is hardwired into their nature sees them excelling at sports. Learning to give and take, to share and to socialize are essential lessons that should be taught from a young age.

The sacred Ram, as shown on a relief from ancient Persepolis

SIGN ASSOCIATIONS

ZODIAC ESSENTIALS

Yin-Yang Yang

Element Fire

Quality Cardinal

Ruling Planet Mars

OTHER AFFINITIES

Body Parts Head, hair, facial features, forehead

Color Red

Country Germany

Flower Honeysuckle

Gemstone Diamond

Metal Iron

Tree Thorn

Weekday Tuesday

An Aries father will encourage his children to play competitive games

ARIES' BLIND SPOT

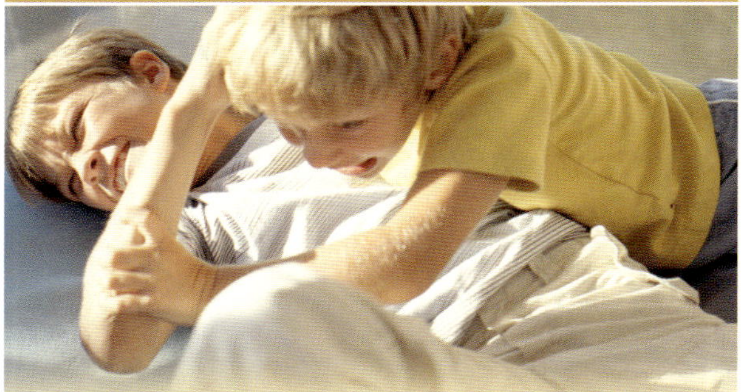

Aries likes boisterous games and may not realize how pushy and irritating he can be

Frankly, Aries people rarely like to share anything with others. What's theirs is theirs. They also want to do what they want to do, when they want to do it, regardless of anyone else. Bold and courageous they may be, but in their rush to be first they can also be rather selfish. Moreover, in being so direct and pushy, they can sometimes forget that others may not be quite as robust. Sometimes, Aries people can be blindly insensitive toward those whom they consider to be in any way weaker than themselves.

ARIES AS A PARENT

Because Aries people believe that children should learn to stand on their own two feet, they expect their youngsters to be independent from a very early age. They enjoy rough and tumble games with their children, and because they want their offspring to be the best, they encourage competitive spirits and are unstinting with praise for sporting achievements. On the whole, Aries takes a robust approach to child rearing. However, in the drive to produce strong, self-reliant, successful children, it's as well to remember that not all youngsters are born to compete, nor does every child see the need to win.

LOVE AND RELATIONSHIPS

It is the direct and confident manner of Aries that immediately comes across to new acquaintances. Open, friendly, and vivacious, Aries is quite an

Mars, the god of war and ruler of Aries

PARTNERS IN LOVE

With a high sex drive, Aries needs an equally passionate partner. Another Aries is a naturally good match, and Gemini can be fun, but the best matches of all are with Leo or Sagittarius.

Aries with:

♈	**Aries**	A partnership filled with excitement	♥♥♥♥
♉	**Taurus**	A battle of wills	♥♥
♊	**Gemini**	An entertaining duo	♥♥♥♥
♋	**Cancer**	This can be a strain	♥♥
♌	**Leo**	Intense passion	♥♥♥♥♥
♍	**Virgo**	Emotionally draining	♥
♎	**Libra**	Requires effort, but can hit the heights	♥♥♥
♏	**Scorpio**	Like being in a pressure cooker	♥♥♥
♐	**Sagittarius**	What an adventure!	♥♥♥♥♥
♑	**Capricorn**	Driven, but in different directions	♥♥♥
♒	**Aquarius**	Surprisingly invigorating	♥♥♥♥
♓	**Pisces**	More trouble than it's worth	♥

Key: ♥ why bother? ♥♥ whenever ♥♥♥ wow ♥♥♥♥ wonderful ♥♥♥♥♥ well hot!

extrovert. In love as in life, he or she is constantly looking for challenge and adventure. The chase, the novelty, the conquering of a quarry, and the excitement of the new are what thrill them about any sexual liaison.

This is not surprising when you consider that this sign is ruled by the planet Mars—positive, powerful, and potent. As the god of war, Mars is a major driving force in the Aries person's life, turning each romantic conquest into a contest in the game of love. In an Aries person's youth, these conquests would be notched as trophies of sexual prowess and success.

There's no doubt that Aries is a passionate lover, and that suitors find this person fiery and hugely romantic. Dynamic and energetic, Aries launches him- or herself heart and soul into each new romance, taking the lead, driving the action, and calling the shots.

In a relationship, Aries is looking for the best. Often, he or she thinks they've found it, only later to be disappointed. It's no secret that compromise lies at the root of all successful relationships. But for Aries, who astrologically are the firstborn, learning the gentle art of sharing and socializing does not come easily. However, when they do finally learn that lesson and are able to truly give their heart and settle down, they prove to be faithful, honest, and good-humored partners. Finding a mate who will keep their interest high and the sex drive sizzling is a must.

ARIES' CAREER

Whatever the line of business, and whether as employers or employees, Aries people launch themselves into projects with huge enthusiasm. Though they can be impulsive, their particular skill lies in their innovative thinking, never afraid to make suggestions or to try something new.

Life Mantra for Aries:

To truly enjoy life is to savor every little detail the universe has to offer

As employees, Aries people like to be given a good deal of autonomy, and prove themselves time and again by using their initiative. They are especially gifted in commercial affairs, such as launching a new product into a competitive marketplace.

It is the very need for independence that suggests an Aries person is at his or her most productive as a manager or, better still, as the overall boss of the company. Aries people are, after all, born leaders and sure of their own abilities. They can be tough masters, but equally they know how to inspire other people to produce the results they want.

SUITABLE CAREERS

- Driver
- Receptionist
- Explorer
- Builder
- Attorney
- Architect
- Engineer
- Sportsman or Woman
- Manager
- Teacher
- Law Enforcer
- Military Personnel

Senior management or even directorship in an architecture or engineering firm would suit an ambitious Aries person

The head is the most important part of the body for Aries

Aries people make no secret of their ambitions. Indeed, they see their own competitive drive as a positive attribute. But success depends not only on launching a great product, but also on maintaining the impulse and staying the course. That's the part that Aries finds difficult.

MONEY MANAGEMENT

Why, given the constant stream of their brilliant ideas, aren't all Aries people extremely rich? Perhaps it is because they are such impulsive spenders, because they live for the now and don't think about tomorrow, and because, let's face it, they just don't follow through. If, as a native of this sign, you learned to be more financially savvy, you practiced conservation, were not tempted by fast food, short cuts, and deals that appear "too good to be true," then you would be able to save more than you spend—and slowly, build yourself up a personal fortune.

BODY & HEALTH

Impatient and impulsive, Aries does tend to live life in the fast lane. People of this sign rush around everywhere, eating at a gallop, and driving at the speed of light. This impatience to get from A to B is the reason why Aries people are so prone to accidents and injuries. Knocks, burns, cuts, bruises, and breaks are typical.

Historically, each sign of the Zodiac rules a part of the anatomy. The part of the body that comes under a sign's rulership is especially noteworthy, either because it is distinctive, or because it is physiologically vulnerable. Aries' rulership is over the head, which explains why so many Aries people suffer with migraine or injure their heads. Because of this, Aries people benefit now and again from a head massage, soothing away the stresses of the day. Even the simple action of brushing hair is therapeutic for an Aries person, helping to slow the alpha waves and calm down his or her thoughts.

FAMOUS ARIES PEOPLE

Leonardo da Vinci
Artist and scientist
born April 15, 1452

Charlie Chaplin
Silent Era performer
born April 16, 1889

Billie Holiday
Jazz singer
born April 7, 1915

Doris Day
Actress born April 3, 1924

Sir Elton John
Singer born March 25, 1947

Quentin Tarantino
Film director born
March 27, 1963

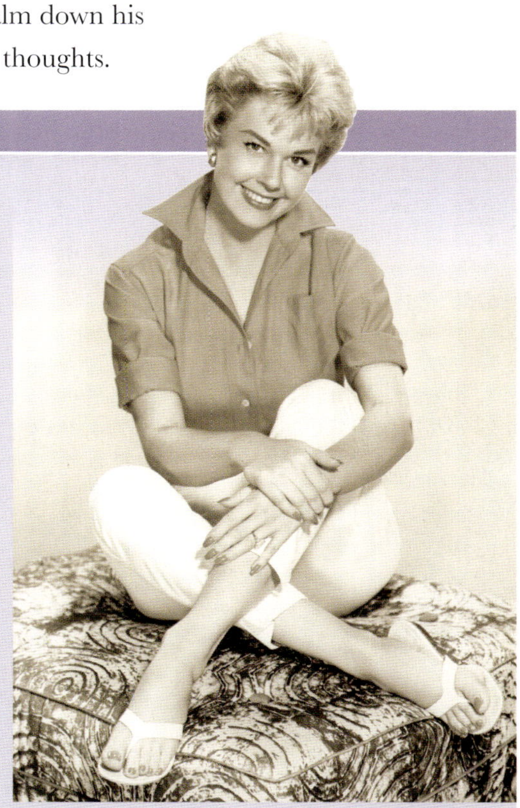

Doris Day

♉ TAURUS

Taurus is a prominent constellation in the night sky, associated in Greek mythology with the white bull-form of Zeus when he wooed Europa. Like the Bull, Taureans are powerful, solid, and usually very calm, but can be roused when sorely provoked.

TAURUS BASICS

Practical, reliable, feet firmly on the ground—this aptly describes Taurus. The sign belongs to the Earth fraternity, making its people solid and stable as a rock. All Earth folk are endowed with resilience and resistance, but Taurean staying-power is legendary and beats everyone else hands down. Taureans are among the most dogged and determined people on the planet and, once setting their mind on an objective, will not give up until reaching the goal.

By nature, Taurus is calm and placid, easy-going, warm-hearted, and patient, and a pleasure to have around. Because Taureans rarely rush anywhere, they have a wonderfully soothing effect on everyone else. Their tolerance is quite amazing. You have to go a long way to reach a Taurean's breaking point. But if pushed that inch too far—if the Taurean is hassled beyond endurance or if someone tries to take something that he or she holds especially precious—watch out. Taurus isn't known as the sign of the Bull for nothing. We all know what happens to a bull when a red rag is waved under its nose…

Security is the biggest need for Taurus. Feeling safe, cozy, and protected is what makes these people happy. Their home is very special, and they spend a lot of time and money making it extra comfortable and luxurious. Most Taureans are green-thumbed, so having access to a yard is important. Left to their own devices, they will putter contentedly around the house, making and creating, or in the yard happily tending to their flowers and vegetables until the sun goes down.

TAURUS

Place in Zodiac Second
Birth Dates April 21–May 21
Symbol The Bull

The Taurean Bull as shown on a 15th-century manuscript from the Mogul Dynasty

WHAT MAKES TAURUS HAPPY?

- People remembering their birthday
- Crunching Fall leaves underfoot
- A meal at the swankiest eatery in town
- Time spent in the yard
- A bottle of fine wine or box of chocolates
- A designer outfit
- A trip on the Orient Express or a weekend at a thermal spa
- Money in the bank!

YOUNG BULLS

Baby Taureans love nothing better than to be cuddled and pampered. Comfort is important to them from the moment they draw their first breath. Being cold, hungry, or wet are outrages that will set them off crying at the top of their lungs. Lots of hugs and plenty of food provide

SIGN ASSOCIATIONS

ZODIAC ESSENTIALS

Yin-Yang Yin

Element Earth

Quality Fixed

Ruling Planet Venus

OTHER AFFINITIES

Body Parts Neck, throat, ears, nose, cheeks, vocal chords

Color Blue

Country Russia

Flower Rose

Gemstone Sapphire

Metal Copper

Tree Apple tree

Weekday Friday

them with the necessary sense of security in which they will develop and thrive. When physically contented, these youngsters are happy little souls who can play quietly on their own for hours on end. Some young Bulls will show a creative flair from a very early age. Others will be more interested in practical construction. For most, however, Nature holds a magical allure.

TAURUS AS A PARENT

Taureans work hard to provide a stable family life. Traditional values are important to them —a nice home, good manners, meals at the right time. They believe in discipline and expect their youngsters to toe the line. However, they are also hugely indulgent, giving the kids plenty of cuddles, cooking their favorite meals, sitting up all night with them through childhood illnesses, helping them with their homework, and—no matter how old they are or how late the hour—always on hand to give

TAURUS' BLIND SPOT

Self-indulgent eating is not one of the Bull's best traits

What's theirs is theirs for Taurus, and that applies to objects as well as people. This sign is possessive in the extreme. The Bull will go into a seething rage if it finds that something, or someone, has been taken from it. On a different note, all Earth signs are hardworking but, given half a chance, Taurus would prefer to put down tools and laze the day away. People of this sign can be self-indulgent and greedy, too, but wouldn't dream of admitting it. Why? Because they are too stubborn!

Nature holds a magical allure for most young Taureans

practical advice. Taureans jealously guard their children's welfare, and woe betide anyone who threatens a hair of their precious heads.

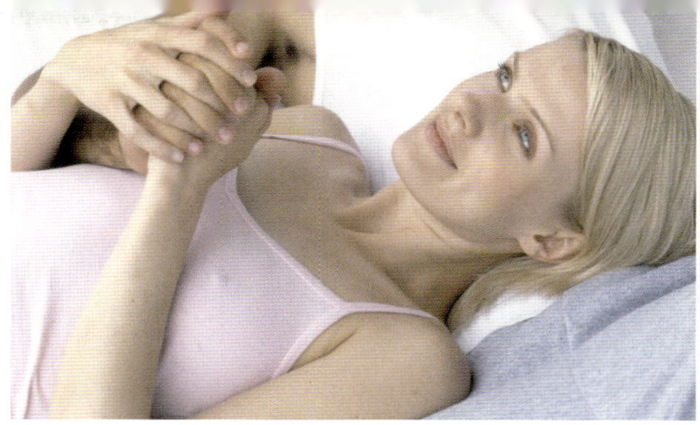

The sense of touch is especially important for Taurus

LOVE AND RELATIONSHIPS

Taureans have an earthy sensuality that makes them very sexy, but they don't flaunt themselves and are not flirtatious. They are, though, very warm and approachable, which attracts people and enables a Taurean, throughout life, to gather and keep a loyal group of friends. Once people get to know a Taurean, it doesn't take them long to discover what a warm-hearted, trustworthy person this is: someone who would do anything to help a friend in need.

People born under this sign are cautious individuals, especially when it comes to giving away their hearts. What they don't do is fall in love at the drop of a hat. They are far too sensible and selective for that. Taureans have high standards, and what they are looking for in a life partner is someone who will be honest, loyal, steadfast, and true. More importantly, they need someone who is a good provider, who will support them through thick and thin, and, especially, someone who shares similar aspirations.

Taureans adore the intimacy of a one-to-one, the shared closeness and the sensual feel of skin on skin—all Taureans are born with an exquisite sense of touch. Precoital massage sends them into sexual ecstasy. They are generous to those they love and good home-makers, too. A comfortable nest is essential, and Taurean larders are always well stocked. Nothing gives them greater pleasure than indulging their family with all the little treats they love best.

PARTNERS IN LOVE

With Venus as their ruling planet, Taureans have the glow of love, sensuousness, and peace. But how will they get on with the other signs of the Zodiac? They will have their work cut out with some.

Taurus with:

♈	**Aries**	Hot and cold ♥♥
♉	**Taurus**	Totally together ♥♥♥♥♥
♊	**Gemini**	Going in different directions ♥
♋	**Cancer**	An erotic combination ♥♥♥♥
♌	**Leo**	A love of the high life unites you ♥♥♥
♍	**Virgo**	Hard-working, successful pair ♥♥♥♥♥
♎	**Libra**	Artistic interests draw you close ♥♥♥
♏	**Scorpio**	A powerful attraction ♥♥♥
♐	**Sagittarius**	Philosophically apart ♥
♑	**Capricorn**	On the same wavelength ♥♥♥♥♥
♒	**Aquarius**	Confrontational ♥♥
♓	**Pisces**	Sensually promising ♥♥♥♥

Key: ♥ why bother? ♥♥ whenever ♥♥♥ wow ♥♥♥♥ wonderful ♥♥♥♥♥ well hot!

A creative streak matched with patience and determination serves Taureans well in a variety of careers, including art

SUITABLE CAREERS

- Singer
- Dancer
- Bank teller
- Financial adviser
- Biologist
- Assessor
- Restaurateur
- Designer
- Artist
- Masseur/masseuse
- Cosmetician
- Horticulturist
- Conservationist

TAUREAN CAREER

One thing's for sure: employers can rely on Taurus. They soon come to realize that, once any Taurean has been given a task, that job will get done. Moreover, Taureans are best left alone to carry out the job in their own way and at their own speed. What they don't like, once they've got started, is to be constantly interrupted, hassled, or pressed to work faster. Extraordinarily determined, Taurus is no quitter, but does like to go at his or her own pace. Once people of this sign have taken on a responsibility, they usually see things through to the bitter end.

As employers themselves, Taureans can be difficult to work for, mainly because they are stubborn and inflexible, and they possess a fiercely traditional, dyed-in-the-wool attitude. Ideally, because of their hard-wired need for long-term security, members of this sign probably feel safer working for an established corporation. Rather than running the business, Taurus is perhaps more comfortable as the number two in the company

Life Mantra for Taurus:

Change opens the door to opportunities and brings fresh experiences into my life

hierarchy. However, whether Taurus is the boss or one of the ranks, his or her caring and considerate nature toward colleagues and coworkers will always come to the fore.

MONEY MANAGEMENT

This sign rules financial affairs—money, earnings, income, and all matters to do with banking. Consequently, Taureans are generally money-oriented in one way or another. Very shrewd in business dealings, they are tough negotiators—few get the better of Taurus when it comes to monetary matters. Whether personally or professionally, Taureans have the knack for successfully managing cash flow. As savers, they would be described as risk-averse, preferring traditional investments and blue-chip companies. They have a good eye for a bargain, however, and acquire possessions that will accrue in value. Material success is important to them, and they make sure there is always enough cash tucked away for that rainy day.

BODY & HEALTH

Few people know that Taurus is the sign of natural beauty. Among the most charming Taurean physical characteristics are dimples in the cheeks. There is also a warm, fecund, wholesomeness about these people that immediately makes them stand out in a crowd.

The typical body silhouette for Taurus is the pear or apple shape. People of this sign find it difficult to keep off unwanted inches. Furthermore, because they would much prefer to curl up in a favorite armchair, flicking through a glossy magazine or reading a coffee-table book of artworks, rather than spending time down at the gym, staying in shape takes a lot of effort.

The neck and throat are the most vulnerable health area for the Bull, and many Taureans regularly develop tonsillitis or hoarseness of the voice. Gargling, hot honey, and lemon drinks, and woolen scarves worn in winter are all great health aids for members of this sign.

FAMOUS TAURUS PEOPLE

Fred Astaire
Dancer born May 10, 1899

Salvador Dali
Painter born May 11, 1904

Sugar Ray Robinson
Boxer born May 3, 1921

Malcolm X
Activist born May 19, 1925

Queen Elizabeth II
British monarch born April 21, 1926

Audrey Hepburn
Actress born May 4, 1929

Barbra Streisand
Singer/actress born April 24, 1942

David Beckham
Soccer star born May 2, 1975

Fred Astaire

GEMINI

Ruled by Mercury, the planet of speed and communication, Gemini is lively and sharp-witted. The symbol of this sign is the Twins, linked with various twins in mythology, especially Castor and Pollux who voyaged with Jason and the Argonauts.

GEMINI BASICS

Gemini is known as a Mutable Air sign *(see page 10)*. A Mutable sign describes someone who is flexible and adaptable. It means that they can bend and bow with events, easily mediate between people, and form a bridge that links the impetus of the Cardinal signs with the practical constructiveness of the Fixed signs. The Air element enhances the intellect. Basically, Gemini is an ideas person. Mentally active, the Geminian has a lively imagination, and is a smart thinker. In fact, these people are razor sharp. They always have a quip to hand and, invariably, the last word, too.

GEMINI

Place in Zodiac Third
Birth Dates May 22–June 22
Symbol The Twins

That Gemini is known as the sign of the Twins is no coincidence. So quick is a Geminian at picking up concepts, so ready with responses, and so fast at getting around—mentally and physically—that you could swear there were two of them. This person is like greased lightning, and slippery as quicksilver. Positive, outgoing, and versatile, Gemini has a low boredom threshold and thrives on variety and change. The wider the circle of acquaintances, and the more on the agenda, the happier is Gemini.

WHAT MAKES GEMINI HAPPY?

- Settling down to a long chat with a friend
- Browsing in a bookstore
- Buying toys for children
- Gossiping in the corridor
- Surfing the Net
- Getting involved in local events
- Sending text messages
- Putting their feet up with a glossy magazine
- Thinking up slogans for a competition

YOUNG GEMINI

Youngsters of this fast and active sign are alert little individuals. From the moment they are born they respond to stimuli all around—noise, light, and sound. That is why it is essential to surround Gemini children with brightly colored toys that will engage their imagination, with music and poetry to delight their ears, and fragrances to tickle their sense of smell.

Geminians learn to speak earlier than most other children. Indeed, once they have found their voice, they hardly stop to draw breath from then on. Life is busy for these confident little youngsters who want to cram as many interests, hobbies, and extracurricular activities as they can into each and every day.

Twins depicted in a 17th-century, Isfahan-style silk panel from Persia

SIGN ASSOCIATIONS

ZODIAC ESSENTIALS

Yin-Yang Yang

Element Air

Quality Mutable

Ruling Planet Mercury

OTHER AFFINITIES

Body Parts Hands, arms, legs, lungs, tongue, nervous system

Color Yellow

Country U.S.

Flower Lily of the Valley

Gemstone Opal

Metal Quicksilver (mercury)

Tree Walnut

Weekday Wednesday

GEMINI'S BLIND SPOT

There's something of the split personality about Gemini. Some would say two-faced. Others call it a Jekyll and Hyde tendency. Chatty and friendly Geminians may appear but, turn around and if it suits them, they can become catty and unpleasant. They're cunning, able to bluff their way out of any difficult situation, even if it means telling a few downright lies. They like to talk so much that they never really stop, even when other people's eyes glaze over. When they want something, they will go around in circles until they get it. Geminians can be copycats, too, passing off other people's original ideas as their own.

GEMINI AS A PARENT

Gemini is the sign of youthfulness. Indeed, Gemini people keep their young looks and lively intelligence well into old age. Parenthood is a joy as it gives them a second chance to relive all the thrills and delights of childhood. They are never happier than when playing games with youngsters, teaching them to count or reading favorite stories at bedtime. They positively encourage their educational activities, helping them to learn, to discover, and to experience all that life has to

The Geminian parent is always eager to play fun, educative games with their child

offer. The generation gap doesn't seem to bother them at all. However, as the brood grows, it's as well to bear in mind the acute sensitivities of the teenager who may prefer that their mom and dad keep a respectful distance, and not try to smudge the gap between parent and child.

PARTNERS IN LOVE

Whether you're already attached or still searching, cosmic combinations hold the clues to your long-term future happiness. Take a look here for the ideal matches for Gemini.

Gemini with:

♈	**Aries**	A great combination	♥♥♥♥
♉	**Taurus**	Too plodding	♥
♊	**Gemini**	Loving, lighthearted, and fun	♥♥♥♥♥
♋	**Cancer**	At odds with each other	♥
♌	**Leo**	Wonderfully entertaining	♥♥♥♥
♍	**Virgo**	Mental touch but little else	♥♥
♎	**Libra**	A sparkling success	♥♥♥♥♥
♏	**Scorpio**	Heavygoing	♥
♐	**Sagittarius**	A good adventure	♥♥♥
♑	**Capricorn**	Hard work	♥♥
♒	**Aquarius**	Sheer magic	♥♥♥♥♥
♓	**Pisces**	Only with masses of give and take	♥♥

Key: ♥ why bother? ♥♥ whenever ♥♥♥ wow ♥♥♥♥ wonderful ♥♥♥♥♥ well hot!

LOVE AND RELATIONSHIPS

Gemini is a wonderfully social and sociable sign. A bubbly extrovert, the Geminian is a people's person. Getting their message across is a high priority for Geminians, and, in fact, something they do extremely well. Compulsive talkers and voracious readers, Gemini people always have plenty to say. They are easy to get along with, highly amusing, and great value at any gathering, party, or social event with a ready wit and funny stories. People are drawn to them, and no wonder—that engaging smile, those affable ways. They seem to know exactly how and when to turn on the charm. That's why it's so easy for them to make friends, and why their address books are bulging at the seams.

The Geminian hunger for constant change, for new stimulation and variety means that they flit from one person to another. Hanging around for too long in one place or in the company of one person will make them restless and bored. This need for constant variety and change can turn young Geminians into consummate flirts. That's the difficulty when it comes to one-on-one intimate relationships—Geminians find it hard to sustain interest with one person for the long term.

There are many people who can capture the heart of a Geminian, but it takes someone special to hold on to it. With this remarkable person who knows how to keep the Geminian amused, when to give plenty of rope and when to rein them in, the Geminian will be happy to forge a partnership that is lighthearted, delightful, and full of fun.

Ever the talker, the Geminian is a great salesperson

GEMINIAN CAREER

The first challenge, when it comes to finding a job, is actually deciding which career path to choose. Having so many different interests, and wanting to dabble in all of them, can mean that Geminians lack a clear focus and direction in life. It has been said about Gemini people that they are Jacks-of-all trades and masters of none. What is for certain is that they have the gift of gab, and thus make superb salesmen and saleswomen.

SUITABLE CAREERS

- Sales
- Teaching
- Information Technology
- Journalism or writing
- Illustration
- Media and TV
- Human Resources
- Postal services
- Clerical or secretarial
- Receptionist

Because a Gemini person tends to shun absolute responsibility, being the overall boss of the company is not ideal. However, the Geminian will shine as manager of a department and be in his or her element as team leader. Gemini's greatest life skill is in communicating with other people. Wherever there is information to collect or disseminate, there will be Gemini. These people like to keep an ear to the ground, stay abreast of the latest news and views, and keep up-to-date with everything that's going on. Working in the media, in journalism, TV, or the field of information technology are ideal paths.

Essentially, though, Gemini people are among the best wheeler-dealers in the business, and because they like to have a finger in many pies, being freelance suits them, especially if they can have a mixed portfolio of jobs.

Life Mantra for Gemini:

I can achieve great things by identifying my priorities and focusing on the task in hand

......

MONEY MANAGEMENT

Gemini can be a worrier when it comes to money, especially if debts have been racked up. It is in the Gemini nature to be whimsical, which means they can be quite frivolous with spending. So it would certainly be to their advantage to make a rule to save a percentage of income no matter what. That way, they will be sure to have a "float" tucked away to spend on that latest "must-have." Luckily, a Geminian can fit into almost any line of work so if cash is ever a serious issue, they should be able to turn to something that guarantees a good wage. Gemini people have plenty of contacts and are so clever at striking deals that they usually end up financially solvent and comfortable sooner or later.

FAMOUS GEMINI PEOPLE

Queen Victoria
British monarch
born May 24, 1819

Marilyn Monroe
Actress born
June 1, 1926

Anne Frank
Jewish writer
born June 12, 1929

Paul McCartney
Singer born
June 18, 1942

Johnny Depp
Actor born
June 9, 1963

Kylie Minogue
Singer born
May 28, 1968

Marilyn Monroe

Getting enough sleep is very important for Gemini people, who use up a lot of energy with their built-in restlessness

BODY & HEALTH

The best health advice to give any Gemini person is to ensure that he or she gets enough sleep. Being so restless, so fidgety, so mentally sharp, all too quickly uses up reserves of nervous energy. Establishing a good routine—time to sit down to a proper meal instead of eating on the hoof, taking regular exercise, getting to bed at a decent hour—will help to boost the Geminian sense of well-being. Getting plenty of fresh air, too, is good because Geminians tend to have respiratory ailments. Shoring up the immune system is essential to ward off colds and chills, which are part and parcel of Geminian susceptibilities, as well as all the other minor bugs that seem to seek them out when they are at their most vulnerable.

♋ CANCER

The name of this sign of the Zodiac derives from the Latin for "crab," and is linked with the legendary crab sent by Hera to distract Hercules in battle. Like the crab, Cancer people like to retreat into a protective shell. They enjoy hearth and home.

CANCER BASICS

Ruled by the Moon and belonging to the Water element immediately reveals Cancer to be a highly emotional being. Water is always associated with the feelings, and therefore, whether male or female, a Cancer person will find emotions washing over them, sometimes quite unexpectedly.

The Crab is a well-chosen symbol, because it describes the character and personality of Cancer in many apt ways. For a start, the crab uses its shell as a protective shelter, just as Cancer people quickly retreat when feeling emotionally vulnerable or under attack. Or, Cancer people attempt to mask their true tenderness behind a bluff exterior by presenting themselves to the world as hard cases, carapace-first, and acting much tougher than they really are.

Then there is the other aspect of the shell. It is where the Crab lives —the house it continuously carries around. For people born under the sign of Cancer, there is nowhere more special than home. Here, they feel safe. Here they pour all their creative energy. Home is their heaven.

Just like the crab who scuttles about on the hot sand one minute and the next pops back inside its shell, there's a dual introverted-extroverted nature to the Cancer personality. When Cancer people feel like it, they are happy to be in the company of others, or one of the crowd. Then there are times when they need to be alone, especially if left to potter around in the house, to spend some contented hours tending the garden, or to cook up something special in the kitchen for the people they love.

CANCER

Place in Zodiac Fourth
Birth Dates June 23–July 23
Symbol The Crab

The Crab, as portrayed in this 19th-century Japanese woodblock print, is a cautious, mood-driven creature

WHAT MAKES CANCER HAPPY?

- Stepping through their own front door
- Photos of loved ones
- A well-stocked refrigerator
- Mom's home cooking
- Little parcels perfectly wrapped
- Visiting country estates
- Browsing in antiques stores
- Family get-togethers
- Walking by the river
- Soaking in a long, hot bath

YOUNG CANCERIANS

Babies born under the influence of the Water element tend to be clingy and emotionally needy. A little Cancerian will form a very close bond with his or her mother—a relationship that remains strong throughout life. Cancer children seem to need more nurturing than most, so plenty of

SIGN ASSOCIATIONS

ZODIAC ESSENTIALS

Yin-Yang Yin
Element Water
Quality Cardinal
Ruling Planet Moon

OTHER AFFINITIES

Body Parts Chest, endocrine system, hormones, stomach, breasts and womb in women
Color White
Country African countries
Flower Lily
Gemstone Pearl
Metal Silver
Tree Palm
Weekday Monday

CANCER'S BLIND SPOT

Moody, moody, moody—and unforgiving, too. Woe betide if someone criticizes a member of their family or, heaven forbid, offends their mother. Cancerians won't forget a slight. Years after the event they'll still rancor over some misdemeanor that everyone else thought trivial and is now long forgotten. Not by the native of the Crab, though! This person has a longer memory than an elephant.

close contact, cuddles, and hugs are appropriate for these tender young souls. As they grow, they develop a passion for gathering and collecting. Seashells, pebbles, stamps, and all manner of memorabilia clutter their rooms. Cooking and gardening are favorite hobbies when young, but, as they progress through school, Cancerian youngsters will excel at history and subjects involving conservation.

CANCER AS A PARENT

Astrologically, not only is Cancer the sign of the home, it is also the sign of the family. Whether as a father or a mother, the Cancer person was born to nurture. So, when youngsters come along, Cancerians rejoice in their parental role, creating a cozy environment in which their little ones will grow and flourish. Cancer women are natural mothers, enjoying the loving closeness of their babies and settling easily into domestic life. Cancer fathers dote on their offspring but must learn not to wrap their children too tightly in a protective shell.

LOVE AND RELATIONSHIPS

Getting to know the Cancer person isn't easy, mainly because this is a sensitive and complex individual. Cancer is always quite contradictory: sunshiny one day, but shy and secretive the next.

Highly emotional and easily hurt, when Cancer people are unsure of their ground they apply the typical Cancerian caution, preferring to hold back until they know the score. Only then will they open up to a stranger or dare to venture forth into territory unknown.

Fidelity is a characteristic prized by Cancer. People of this sign are among the most loyal in the Zodiac. Once they give their hearts, they become highly supportive companions,

Domestic bliss is the key to happiness for Cancer

working hard for their partners, family, and homes. Female Cancer people are especially caring and maternal, while male Crabs are a great catch, being generally homely individuals who like to cook and share in the household duties. Whether male or female, the Cancer person will be hugely romantic and will believe in respect, courtesy, and old-fashioned values.

Unfortunately, Cancer is a martyr to mood swings. Keep an eye on the lunar phases and notice how these affect the Cancer person, changing their feelings as the moon waxes and wanes. The full moon effects are particularly potent, making Cancer people extra elated or extra grumpy, depending on what's happening around them at the time. A partner will soon get to recognize the signs, and if he or she is smart, will leave Cancer alone until the crabbedness has passed and is replaced by that lovely smile again.

One thing to bear in mind—all Cancer people, whether male or female, are close to their mothers. While Cancer women will want to share their lives with a strong yet sensitive partner, the male of the species simply wants someone who is just like his dear, sweet mother.

PARTNERS IN LOVE

Looking for long-lasting love, Cancer? Then avoid Aries and Gemini. Take a look at your star ratings to see where your true destiny lies. Other Yin signs *(see page 10)* are definitely the best for Cancer.

Cancer with:

♈	**Aries**	Better at a distance	♥♥
♉	**Taurus**	Emotionally rewarding	♥♥♥♥
♊	**Gemini**	Different needs	♥
♋	**Cancer**	Totally together	♥♥♥♥♥
♌	**Leo**	An interesting relationship	♥♥♥
♍	**Virgo**	A very strong union	♥♥♥♥
♎	**Libra**	An off-key relationship	♥
♏	**Scorpio**	A passionate pair	♥♥♥♥♥
♐	**Sagittarius**	Your differences will grate	♥♥
♑	**Capricorn**	You're good for each other	♥♥♥♥
♒	**Aquarius**	Conflicts galore	♥♥
♓	**Pisces**	A blissful combination	♥♥♥♥♥

Key: ♥ why bother? ♥♥ whenever ♥♥♥ wow ♥♥♥♥ wonderful ♥♥♥♥♥ well hot!

SUITABLE CAREERS

- Historian
- Agriculturalist
- Landscape gardener
- Shopkeeper
- Chef
- Archivist
- Conservationist
- Archeologist
- Builder
- Architect
- Personnel manager
- Teacher
- Child minder

CANCERIAN CAREER

Contented inside their own shells, Cancer folk of both sexes tend to be stay-at-homes. The chance to turn a spare room into an office and either to work from home, go freelance, or become totally self-employed is ideal. Whether working for a company or for themselves, Cancer people are hardworking, trustworthy, and loyal. Give the Crab a task to do, a team of people to manage or even the keys to the building, and the boss is assured that all will be accomplished, safely and securely.

Cancerian employers care about the welfare and well-being of the workforce and are respected for their kindly, benign ways. They treat people with the same courtesy, civility, and good

Life Mantra for Cancer:

Exploring the unfamiliar opens up new sensations, which add richness and color to my life

Archeology will satisfy a Cancerian's natural interests in history and conservation

The ever-changing Moon adds to mood swings for Cancer

manners that they expect to receive. Whatever the line of work, Cancer's tenacious memory comes in handy for recalling facts, figures, names, or faces from the past. However, it is undoubtedly the Crab's intuition that is at the core of its success in business and that enables Cancer to stay ahead of the game.

MONEY MANAGEMENT

Perhaps it is that prescience of Cancer that guides people of the sign in financial affairs. Or perhaps it is the retentive memory and love of history that enables them to recognize repeating patterns of events. Whichever, when it comes to money, they are shrewd and calculating, and somehow avoid falling into the pitfalls that lure less astute signs. Indeed, Cancer people have a real knack with money and are able steadily to accumulate comfortable resources. Good fortune seems to follow them about, especially when they are shopping, bargain-hunting, or involved in forging deals.

When it comes to savings, Cancer tends to be risk-averse, preferring to invest in old-established companies with cast-iron pedigrees. Slow but sure is the motto when it comes to managing investments.

BODY & HEALTH

Members of the three Water signs—Pisces, Scorpio, and Cancer—tend to be driven by their emotions more than the other nine. Given that Cancer is also ruled by the ever-changing Moon, it is little wonder, then, that Cancer people are prone to mood swings. Worry can get the better of them. They are champions at making mountains out of molehills, letting anxieties build up so much that at times they come close to nervous exhaustion. It is this very tendency to worry that can aggravate the Cancerian stomach, which is the sign's anatomical weak link. Any problem seems immediately to create nervous indigestion, heartburn, nausea, and gastric ulcers. Learning to stay on an even keel, find ways to unwind and worry less, and to eat sensibly are essential. Water sports are suitable, as are walks by the sea.

Fortunately, Cancer people are no more statistically likely to develop cancer diseases than those born under other signs of the Zodiac.

FAMOUS CANCER PEOPLE

Gaius Julius Caesar
Roman leader
born July 12, 100 BC

Marc Chagall
Painter born July 7, 1887

Nelson Mandela
South African leader
born July 18, 1918

Sylvester Stallone
Actor born July 6, 1946

Camilla Parker Bowles
British duchess
born July 17, 1947

Tom Cruise
Actor born July 3, 1962

Nelson Mandela

♌ LEO

Leo is the fifth sign of the Zodiac, a large constellation in the night sky, with many bright stars and galaxies within. It is a Fire sign associated with glorious heat and power. Leo people are essentially extrovert and they have a great zest for life.

LEO BASICS

Proud and big-hearted, Leo is symbolized very aptly by the Lion. It is also ruled by the Fire element and forms part of the group of Zodiac signs that are known as Fixed *(see page 10)*. All this adds up to a charismatic individual with a positive, purposeful personality.

Being born under Leo means that, like the Lion, these individuals are noted for their courage. In the wild, the lion is the king of beasts, and Leo people, too, have a strong sense of nobility running through their blood. There is something quite majestic and grand about them. Even the way they carry themselves—male Leos walking tall, females with their heads held high—reflects this distinction. If truth be told, Leos do actually believe they were born to rule.

It is obvious that Leo's celestial ruler is the Sun itself because Leos radiate a wonderful warmth. They are gloriously colorful and dramatic—true extroverts who like to live life to the full. Just as all the planets revolve around the Sun, Leos like to be at the center of whatever is going on. In fact, they court the limelight, never happier than when in the spotlight, center stage of the action, and at the heart of the social circle.

Leo is a fortunate sign and, time and again, Leo people will discover just how lucky they are. They may take risks but, like the big cat that represents the sign, they somehow always manage to land on their feet.

LEO

Place in Zodiac Fifth
Birth Dates July 24–August 23
Symbol The Lion

WHAT MAKES LEO HAPPY?

- People pampering and making a fuss over them
- Dining in swanky restaurants
- A large, ornate, Venetian mirror
- Anything gold
- Being mistaken for a movie star
- A glass (or three) of vintage champagne
- A big hug from someone special in their life
- Winning!

YOUNG LEOS

Little Leos thrive on attention. Laugh at their jokes, encourage their japes, praise their antics, and they will put on a bigger and better show next time. Even as tiny tots, Leos respond to an audience. Lively and vivacious, they are natural performers and will do almost anything to grab the limelight. These youngsters develop early, often showing precocious talent. At school, they soon gravitate toward the Arts although many

Lion statue outside New York Public Library

SIGN ASSOCIATIONS

ZODIAC ESSENTIALS

Yin-Yang Yang

Element Fire

Quality Fixed

Ruling Planet Sun

OTHER AFFINITIES

Body Parts Heart, spine, back, blood circulation system, shoulder blades, waist

Color Flame orange

Country Italy

Flower Marigold

Gemstone Ruby

Metal Gold

Tree Bay

Weekday Sunday

Leo men are children at heart

LEO'S BLIND SPOT

Proud, warm-hearted, generous, and enthusiastic. That's the text book description of people born under this sign. However, all these good qualities have their flipside, too, which show up only too obviously on a bad day. For example, that pride can so easily turn into arrogance and conceit. Warmhearted and generous? Watch how, when unchecked, these tendencies become pompous, patronizing, over-the-top, and lacking in good taste. And is that enthusiastic streak just a mite too bossy, too controlling, too demanding, too dominant? Well, no one's perfect. Not even a Leo.

excel in drama. However, teenage Leos can shine in almost any subject just as long as they are given the right encouragement and rewards.

LEO AS A PARENT

Any Leo has a natural ability to communicate easily with young people, so becoming a parent should not present too many difficulties. Leos can take noisy children in their stride and they join in with the fun and mischief because, fundamentally, they are children at heart themselves.

Leo parents involve themselves in their children's development and interests at every stage of their upbringing. Family achievements are important to them. Consequently, the Leo parent will encourage his or her youngsters to strive hard in life and to aim high.

LOVE AND RELATIONSHIPS

Magnanimous, flamboyant, warm, and sunny: how can anybody resist you, Leo?

There's something rather golden and heroic about a male Leo that has women falling at his feet. Female Leos, meanwhile, exude fabulous pheromones that draw men like moths to a candle flame. The Lion is born with magnetic qualities that, quite frankly, leave everyone else in the shade.

Leo people are blessed with immense charm and charismatic personalities that attract admirers to their sides. So finding a mate usually isn't too difficult. These people are so romantic, loving with a fiery passion and giving themselves heart and soul to their lovers. Good looks are important; a generous spirit to match is also essential. Romancing Leos with overblown gestures will win their hearts. Though Leo people like to tease and flirt, once they have given their hearts, they remain constant and true.

PARTNERS IN LOVE

Leo is one of the most charming and attractive signs, and there is usually no problem for a Leo person to find potential suitors. Long-term suitability with other signs is summarized below.

Leo with:

♈	**Aries**	Hot, spicy passion	♥♥♥♥♥
♉	**Taurus**	Promising pleasures	♥♥♥
♊	**Gemini**	Lively and constantly stimulating	♥♥♥♥
♋	**Cancer**	Sweet and romantic	♥♥♥
♌	**Leo**	Fiery but so dramatic	♥♥♥♥♥
♍	**Virgo**	Argumentative	♥
♎	**Libra**	A very stylish couple	♥♥♥♥
♏	**Scorpio**	Steamy but challenging	♥♥♥
♐	**Sagittarius**	A powerful attraction	♥♥♥♥♥
♑	**Capricorn**	Ultimately disappointing	♥♥
♒	**Aquarius**	Divided opinions	♥♥
♓	**Pisces**	Good for each other	♥♥♥

Key: ♥ why bother? ♥♥ whenever ♥♥♥ wow ♥♥♥♥ wonderful ♥♥♥♥♥ well hot!

Romantic Leos

Whether the male or the female in a relationship, Leo likes to be the boss. Yes, the Lion can be vain and egocentric, exploding into a rage now and again, or going into a deep sulk when others seem to be ignoring him or her. However, those bad moods don't last long, and though Leo can roar like the proverbial lion, the row will soon be forgotten and Leo will go back to purring like a contented cat, all smiles and playfulness again.

Leo is a big personality, with a big heart, a wonderful sense of humor, and a great bundle of fun. Yes, totally and completely irresistible.

LEO'S CAREER

A born leader, Leo's natural predisposition is to rise to be the boss. So whatever line of work people of this sign find themselves in, they aim to reach the top. Even when they first set foot on the career ladder, it doesn't take them long to gravitate to a position of seniority, to be chosen to head up projects or to be made leader of the group. Managing their own department suits them well. But being the outright chief, the head honcho, the governor of the company suits them even better. Let's face it, Leo is never happier than when in charge! From the outset, the Lion is drawn either toward a glittery, glamorous career or to an executive position in a prestigious company.

SUITABLE CAREERS

- Actor
- Director
- Beautician
- Fashion designer
- Executive
- Performer
- Agent
- Teacher
- Obstetrician
- Demonstrator
- Celebrity
- Leisure management

Life Mantra for Leo:

My heart reflects Mother Nature's bounty; in sharing I find joy

In general, members of this sign do not function well in lowly jobs or in situations where they are in service to others. Being ignored, sidelined, or passed over at promotion is a mortal blow. To give his or her best, Leo needs constant reassurance, regular compliments, good

Leo likes to be the highflier

rewards, and frequent pats on the back. As employers, the innate kindness and consideration of Leos toward their workforce wins them respect. Whether it's their charm, persuasiveness, or sheer enthusiasm that rubs off on others, Leo people seem to have the knack of knowing just how to get people to do what they want.

MONEY MANAGEMENT

Generous to a fault, Leo people are always the first to put their hands in their pockets when someone comes around with the collection box, whether for charity or for a workmate's leaving party. Again, Leos are always ready to help a friend in need, or to buy treats for those they love. Money, for people of this sign, is something to be enjoyed. Splashing it around makes them happy and, if buying a round of drinks for their colleagues after work makes them a little more popular, well, that's okay by them.

Leo people belong, arguably, to the most extravagant sign of the Zodiac. Gifts are usually lavish, both for other people and for themselves. Leos especially find jewelry and designer clothes irresistible. They are drawn to the high life, to opulence, and to five-star everything. Fortunately, they seem able to earn enough to keep themselves and their families in this grand style. However, learning to save more than what is spent would be a good lesson to acquire as early in life as possible.

BODY & HEALTH

Leos have big appetites. Not just of the culinary sort but physically, emotionally, and intellectually, they have a huge gusto for living life to the full. They simply cannot do anything by halves. Whether it's at work or at play, with a group of strangers or among people they know and love, these big-hearted folk push themselves to extremes in their desire to achieve and to be the best. Unfortunately, it is this very drive to succeed that can put a strain on the Leo heart.

If you belong to this sign, it is as well to be aware of the Leo susceptibilities, which are essentially associated with the coronary system, chest, and circulation. Also linked with the sign of the Lion are the back and spinal column. Take extra care of these areas when you're working out in the gym, and avoid putting undue strain on your back when lifting heavy objects.

As in every aspect of life, balance and moderation are essential, especially for such a competitive creature as the Lion. People born under Leo should try to eat sensibly, exercise regularly, and head for the fresh air—and, of course, the sun—as often as they possibly can.

FAMOUS LEO PEOPLE

Napoleon Bonaparte
French commander born August 15, 1769

Amelia Earhart
Aviator born July 24, 1897

Gene Kelly
Actor and dancer born August 23, 1912

Fidel Castro
Cuban leader born August 13, 1926

Jackie Kennedy Onassis
First Lady born July 28, 1929

Madonna
Entertainer and icon born August 16, 1958

Madonna

♍ VIRGO

A Yin, or feminine, sign, Virgo is symbolized by the Maiden and associated with a number of goddesses in mythology, including Athena, Hygieia, and the virgin daughter of Zeus. Much about this sign relates to perfection, purity, and cleanliness.

VIRGO BASICS

Mentally, Virgo is meticulous. Here is one of the most discerning minds in the universe. Accurate, analytical, and discriminative—so sharp is Virgo's intellectual acuity that he or she can spot flaws at a hundred paces. The sign is ruled by Mercury, the speedy little planet that sharpens the thinking processes and keeps Virgo on the go. Virgo also belongs to the Earth element, which endows people of the sign with practical ability. They may be fast, but they keep their feet on the ground at all times. The Earth element implies commonsense, manual dexterity, and, especially, a strong sense of realism. Solid and sensible, Virgo is nobody's fool.

VIRGO

Place in Zodiac Sixth
Birth Dates August 24–September 23
Symbol The Maiden

Portrait of a maiden by Louis Weldon Hawkins (1849–1910)

Virgos abhor mess. This is not to say that all Virgos are fastidiously tidy in every way, but they always prefer order to chaos. Virgo is known as "the sign of service," and Virgo individuals are never happier than when in service. Patient, caring, and eager to help, their mission in life seems to revolve around attending to the needs of others. It is worth stopping to consider just what a Virgo's partner, children, family, and even the community at large would do without that Virgo.

WHAT MAKES VIRGO HAPPY?

- A job well done
- Coming across a field of ripened corn
- A rainbow after the storm
- Crisp linen sheets scented with lavender
- A bonsai tree
- A rack of homeopathic remedies
- The latest board game
- An immaculate kitchen with sparkling utensils
- A pet cat sleeping in the sun

YOUNG VIRGOS

Familiarity is important for Virgo babies who thrive on routine. Take them away from their regular surroundings and everyday activities, and they will start to fret. These are intelligent little beings, following the adults around with their eyes and copying what their moms, dads, and siblings do. As they grow, they are eager to learn and in a hurry to apply their knowledge. At school, they win marks for neat handwriting, for manual skills, and for mathematics.

Virgo children are shy individuals who need sensitive encouragement to believe in themselves and develop their talents. Right through their teens and even as young adults, this natural diffidence often means they are slow to make friends.

♍ VIRGO

SIGN ASSOCIATIONS

ZODIAC ESSENTIALS

Yin-Yang Yin

Element Earth

Quality Mutable

Ruling Planet Mercury

OTHER AFFINITIES

Body Parts Abdomen, small intestines, diaphragm, gall bladder, nerve sheaths

Color Terra-cotta

Country Brazil

Flower Forget-me-not

Gemstone Agate

Metal Nickel

Tree Hazel

Weekday Wednesday

VIRGO'S BLIND SPOT

Both male and female Virgos can be harshly critical. This may be the sign of the Virgin, but their sharp tongues could wither a saint! So fussy, fastidious, and exacting are they, that living with these people can be like living on a razor's edge. Nothing is ever good enough, and no one ever comes up to the mark. That is because the mark is so high that it is virtually impossible to reach. Make a mistake and Virgo won't hesitate to point it out to you, and quite bluntly, too. Virgos are not renowned for their sensitivity to those they consider to be their inferior.

Virgo incessantly points out other people's mistakes

A certain shyness stops Virgos from spontaneously expressing their feelings

A Virgo father will heavily involve himself in his child's education

VIRGO AS A PARENT

Virgo parents love their children deeply and work hard for their families. Household discipline is important, so that meals are served on time, bedrooms tidied, and homework completed before leisure activities begin. Virgo fathers and mothers throw themselves wholeheartedly into teaching their youngsters life skills. Consequently, children of Virgo parents are usually very advanced for their age. However, these parents can be overly critical when they find fault, which can be discouraging for the more sensitive child.

PARTNERS IN LOVE

Not the easiest Zodiac sign to catch, Virgo might back away from a relationship in fear of criticism or rejection from the other party. The likely matches with other signs are shown here.

Virgo with:

♈	**Aries**	Exhausting	♥
♉	**Taurus**	A happy and supportive pair	♥♥♥♥♥
♊	**Gemini**	Chatty, but is it the same language?	♥♥
♋	**Cancer**	A cozy twosome	♥♥♥♥
♌	**Leo**	Different ethos, different ideas	♥
♍	**Virgo**	You're a mirror image of each other	♥♥♥♥♥
♎	**Libra**	Conflicts galore	♥♥
♏	**Scorpio**	Strongly in tune together	♥♥♥♥
♐	**Sagittarius**	Not a lot in common	♥
♑	**Capricorn**	A match truly blessed	♥♥♥♥♥
♒	**Aquarius**	Intellectual link but little else	♥♥
♓	**Pisces**	On different planes	♥♥

Key: ♥ why bother? ♥♥ whenever ♥♥♥ wow ♥♥♥♥ wonderful ♥♥♥♥♥ well hot!

LOVE AND RELATIONSHIPS

There is something about Virgos that makes them hold back. Being such perfectionists themselves, they may worry that others won't find them attractive. So they argue in their own minds that it's safer not to get involved in the first place rather than having to suffer the pain of rejection. Sometimes it is that very few people can actually match Virgoan standards of excellence. Therefore it takes Virgos a while to find Mr. or Ms. Right. In their hunt, however, they have quite a wicked sense of humor. Virgos are especially gifted in clever put-down lines! They seek out intelligent people who are drawn to the Virgo wit and relish the challenge of unlocking the Virgo heart. Virgos are not the most abandoned lovers in the Zodiac, but with the right partner, they can learn to relax and enjoy themselves. For those they love, no sacrifice is ever too big. Virgos will devote themselves tirelessly in doing all the little things they know will please their partners most.

Life Mantra for Virgo:

To truly love others, I must first learn to love myself

A job, such as being a veterinarian, will perfectly suit Virgo

VIRGOAN CAREER

Hard-working and high-achieving, Virgo is an asset for any employment sector in which he or she chooses to make a career. Very often, it is the service industries that attract. Moreover, because health and hygiene are of particular interest to Virgos, the world of medicine or the caring professions seem to be a natural environment for their talents. Doctors, nurses, veterinarians, and all manner of ancillary personnel found in hospitals and clinics often come from the Virgo pool. In other fields, the discerning eye of Virgo—that ability to spot the tiniest mistake—will make them invaluable as an editor, auditor, or computer analyst. Virgo's attention to detail and problem solving skills are second to none.

Although Virgos are capable of commanding quiet authority, their tendency to worry suggests that being employed in a company rather than being their own boss provides them with peace of mind. In fact, Virgos make excellent employees.

SUITABLE CAREERS

- Accountant
- Computer analyst
- Editor
- Doctor
- Technician
- Inspector
- Hygienist
- Recorder
- Secretary
- Steward
- Researcher
- Teacher
- Veterinarian

They have the knack of picking up skills and knowledge at a glance—especially where tasks are essentially practical or manually-based. Their intelligence, willingness, and in-built sense of responsibility mean they can be left alone to work without direct supervision, which is a boon to any boss.

Wherever they work, Virgos are never afraid to voice their opinions. On the other hand, so as not to alienate their colleagues, they should endeavor to ensure their comments don't come across as negative criticism.

FAMOUS VIRGO PEOPLE

Leo Tolstoy
Russian novelist
born August 28, 1828

Jesse James
Outlaw born September 5, 1847

Mother Theresa
Nobel Peace Prize winner
born August 27, 1910

Ray Charles
Jazz musician born
September 23, 1932

Sophia Loren
Actress born
September 20, 1934

Cameron Diaz
Actress born August 30, 1972

Ray Charles

MONEY MANAGEMENT

One thing a Virgo doesn't do is splash the cash. Why would they when their needs are so modest? Sensible and cautious, a Virgo man or woman will always be careful about spending and will invariably think about the future before opening up the wallet or handing over the plastic. Basically, Virgos are prudent. Gambling doesn't appeal and they certainly wouldn't dream of investing their capital in risky deals. As with all Earth signs, they know how to manage their money shrewdly. Carefully, steadily, and securely, they put more than enough by for that proverbial rainy day.

BODY & HEALTH

People born at this time of year tend in general to be health conscious—which isn't surprising because Virgo is known as "the sign of health." Many Virgos, in fact, take a keen interest in fitness and well-being, spending a good deal of time thinking and reading about diet and nutrition. If you belong to this Zodiac sign you'll understand why nutrition is such an obsession—your digestive system! For this is Virgo's anatomical weak link. Having a delicate stomach can make Virgos fussy, sometimes even downright faddish, eaters. They suffer if they indulge in too much rich food. Irritable bowel syndrome, dyspepsia, bowel problems, colitis, and gastroenteritis are typically associated with this sign. Sooner or later a Virgo must realize that his or her system rebels against junk foods but that they will thrive on natural whole foods, plenty of fresh fruit and vegetables, cereals, and organic products.

Virgos are born worriers. Their tendency to fuss and fret means that not only do they find it hard to relax, but in turn this sets up a vicious cycle which again affects their stomach. Sticking to a good routine, a sound nutritional regimen, and getting plenty of gentle exercise—walking or playing tennis perhaps—keeps a Virgo well in both body and mind.

LIBRA

Affable, tolerant, and broad-minded, Libra is known as the peacemaker of the Zodiac. The name is Latin for "balance," and the symbol is the Scales. This sign is ruled by Venus and linked with the goddesses Aphrodite, Themis, Atalanta, and others.

LIBRA BASICS

Air is Libra's ruling element *(see page 10)*, which endows people of this sign with an intellectual approach to life. Like Gemini and Aquarius—the other signs belonging to the Air group—Librans are social and sociable. The ability to communicate clearly is among their salient skills.

LIBRA

Place in Zodiac Seventh
Birth Dates September 24–October 23
Symbol The Scales

Perhaps it is because Libra is ruled by that classic beauty Venus that Libran women are so chic and the men so suave. Even when dressed down in jeans and a jersey, a Libran will still manage to exude a polished stylishness. Whatever their age or gender, there is a timeless elegance about them. Again it is Venus's influence that blesses them with refined tastes. Cultured and sophisticated, Librans have an exquisite eye for beautiful objects, for fine clothes and expensive furnishings. In life, they strive for balance, symmetry, calm, harmony, and above all, beauty. A messy environment, displeasing aspect, or rundown area are, for a Libran, to be avoided.

Belonging to this sign means that you have the ability to see both sides of the story. While this enables you to appreciate the other person's point of view, it complicates matters especially when it comes to making personal choices. Weighing up the pros and cons, assessing the situation from all angles, and attempting to achieve a balanced decision not only takes an inordinate amount of time, but often results in deadlock. No wonder, then, that Librans are considered indecisive.

WHAT MAKES LIBRA HAPPY?

- Good manners
- Being the guest of honor at an elegant dinner party
- Light streaming through a stained-glass window
- Throwing confetti at the bride and groom
- Visiting an art gallery
- Reading *Vogue* magazine
- A new silk tie for him or a silk scarf for her
- Watching the sunset
- Strolling arm-in-arm with their lover

YOUNG LIBRANS

Little Librans of both sexes are good-looking and highly photogenic, even as babies. They get on well with other children and have no difficulty in making friends. At school, their fair-minded, easygoing natures make them popular among both their peers and teachers. Though not drawn to contact sports, these youngsters can excel at the gentler or more graceful physical activities such as gymnastics, skating, or skiing. Librans are innately

The Scales of Libra, as shown in a Roman mosaic dating from the 3rd century BC

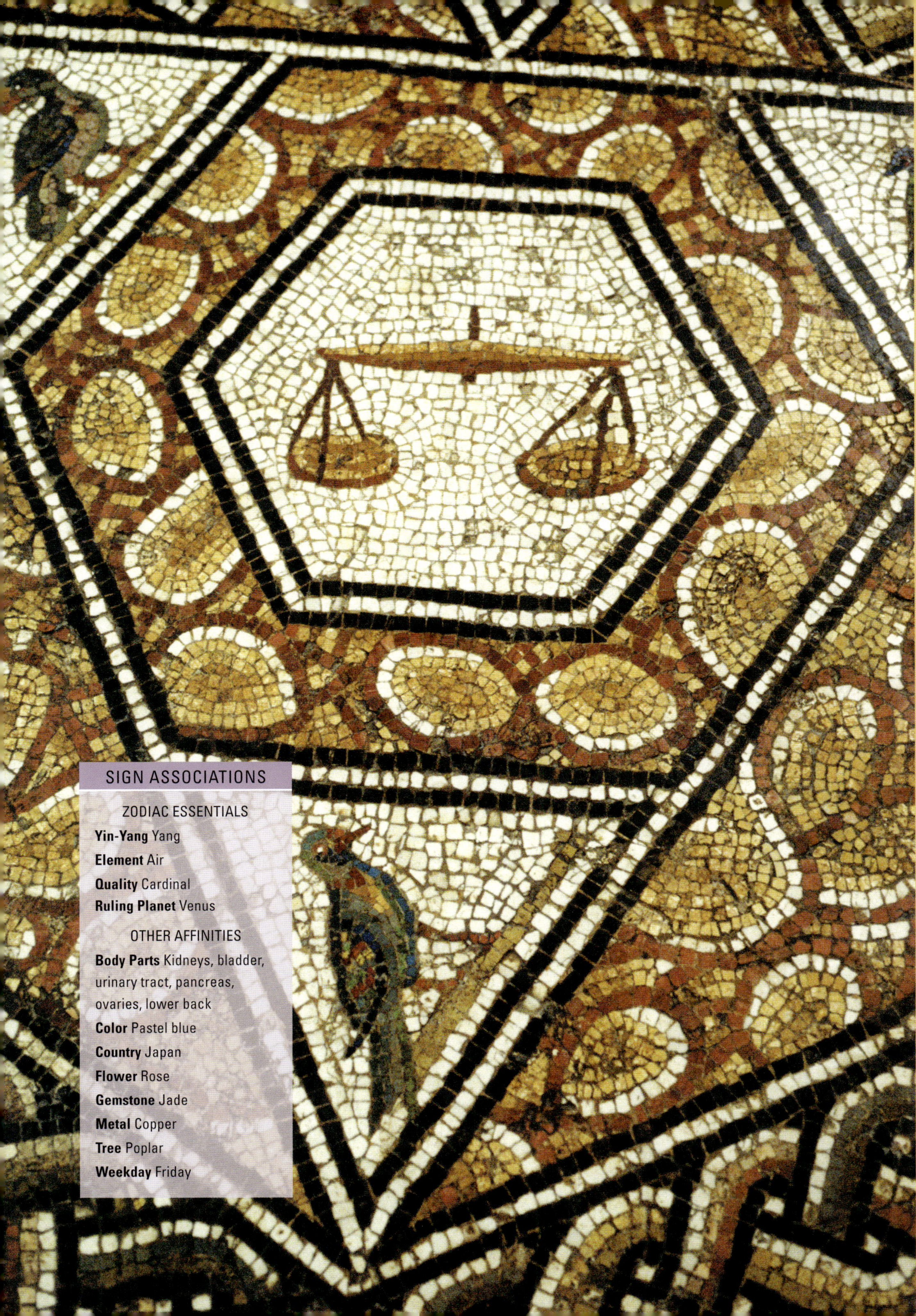

SIGN ASSOCIATIONS

ZODIAC ESSENTIALS

Yin-Yang Yang
Element Air
Quality Cardinal
Ruling Planet Venus

OTHER AFFINITIES

Body Parts Kidneys, bladder, urinary tract, pancreas, ovaries, lower back
Color Pastel blue
Country Japan
Flower Rose
Gemstone Jade
Metal Copper
Tree Poplar
Weekday Friday

LIBRA'S BLIND SPOT

Looks, image, presentation—sometimes Librans can go overboard for the superficial. They can be taken in by grooming and classy clothes without really stopping to examine the true personality underneath. They can easily charm other people with their winning ways, but on a bad day they can take things too far, coming across as downright smarmy and cheesy. Their tendency to sit on the fence can be infuriating. They walk away from difficult or messy situations, leaving other people to mop up behind them. Also, they are so very, very lazy.

artistic, something that is evident from a very early age. They are also quite indolent, however, exerting only as much effort as is necessary to get by. For this reason, any early promise that emerges during these formative years, whether for music, art, design, or whatever, should be judiciously encouraged with balanced discipline in order to hone their skills for the future. If not, these little laid-back Librans may remain amateur dilettantes throughout their lives instead of the true professionals they deserve to become.

LIBRA AS A PARENT

Parents of this sign can be indulgent toward their children, spending lavishly on clothes, toys, education, and general needs. They encourage all creative and cultural interests, taking their youngsters here, there, and everywhere to dancing lessons, musical events, exhibitions, and shows.

The children of a Libran will be taken to dancing lessons and musical events

Libra is an asset at the dinner party

Libran males are not natural hands-on fathers with newborns and prefer to leave the messy diaper stage to their partners. They will come into their own when the children reach school age. Libran parents believe in pleasant manners and teach their offspring respect for other people. They delight in family life but abhor quarrels. As a consequence, they would rather give in to their children's demands than get embroiled in a row. Dishing out punishment is another no-go area for the Libran parent, who usually delegates this to their partner.

PARTNERS IN LOVE

Whether male or female, Libra is made for love. People of this sign have a romantic notion of what relationships are about and really thrive when settled with a partner. Check here for pairing potentials.

Libra with:

♈	**Aries**	Rough with the smooth ♥♥♥
♉	**Taurus**	Unusual but so interesting ♥♥♥
♊	**Gemini**	Absolutely sublime ♥♥♥♥♥
♋	**Cancer**	A long shot ♥
♌	**Leo**	Sheer enjoyment ♥♥♥♥
♍	**Virgo**	Hard going ♥♥
♎	**Libra**	So suave ♥♥♥♥♥
♏	**Scorpio**	Troubled waters ♥♥
♐	**Sagittarius**	A light-hearted pair ♥♥♥♥
♑	**Capricorn**	At odds in many ways ♥♥
♒	**Aquarius**	Fabulous match ♥♥♥♥♥
♓	**Pisces**	Almost a fairytale ♥♥♥

Key: ♥ why bother? ♥♥ whenever ♥♥♥ wow ♥♥♥♥ wonderful ♥♥♥♥♥ well hot!

LOVE AND RELATIONSHIPS

Librans are never short of friends, because they are so charming, amiable, and, above all, good listeners. People know that Libra will give a rounded point of view. A Libran is a great asset at any dinner party: a knowledgeable speaker with interesting things to say.

What every true-blooded Libran yearns for is to bond with a soulmate. They always have a pool of admirers from which to choose, but making that choice is difficult! Librans are notorious for letting many a potential suitor slip through the net simply because they are too slow in making up their minds.

Arguments will deeply upset a Libran, who will prefer to acquiesce to all demands in order to avoid a scene. Perhaps it is for this reason that Libran men are sometimes thought to be henpecked. Female Librans are very feminine and adore making a beautiful home and looking up to a strong, handsome partner. But if the going ever gets too tough for either sex, Librans are apt to find the quickest escape route out.

To be a judge is perfect for Libra

LIBRAN CAREER

Libra's brilliance lies in arbitration. Balancing information, being the go-between, and bringing factions together—that is where they excel. The legal profession suits them well, such as being an attorney, lawyer, barrister, or judge. Tact is one of Libra's qualities, thus many members of this sign find themselves naturally gravitating to jobs in the government or diplomatic corps. The Arts are another big draw. Many connoisseurs, designers, and musicians are of this sign. The Libra person's exquisite eye can successfully take someone into the beauty business or the world of luxury goods. Wherever Libra starts in a career, he or she soon rises up the ladder, invariably dealing with people at a very high level. However, the working environment and colleagues matter significantly to a Libran's overall job satisfaction, achievement, and well-being. To thrive at work and become successful, Librans should avoid overly competitive situations, uncongenial surroundings, or disagreeable, aggressive colleagues. Teamed up with the right people in the right place, Libra usually goes far.

SUITABLE CAREERS

- Agent
- Graphic artist
- Textile designer
- Fashion designer
- Interiors designer
- Landscape designer
- Beautician
- Art dealer
- Liaison officer
- Editor
- Diplomat
- Legal clerk
- Judge

MONEY MANAGEMENT

Librans adore shopping. You won't find any people of this sign in a thrift store, nor are they the sort to fritter away money on incidentals. They have expensive tastes and like designer labels and the best of everything. Their home, clothes, and pastimes certainly don't come cheap. On the other hand, Librans are at least prepared to save up for those choice items. Fortunately, they are capable of commanding a good salary. Luckier still, they have the knack of attracting rich and powerful people who can open doors to financial opportunities. One way or another, Librans are able to manage their cash intelligently and always seem to have enough to satisfy their expensive needs.

BODY & HEALTH

The keys to Libra's well-being are harmony and equilibrium. Keeping the system in tune—not too little, not too much, not too acid, not too alkaline, not too active, not too passive—is crucial for physical, emotional, and psychological health. Upset this delicate equilibrium and Libra's hormonal balance will be thrown out of kilter. In turn, this can affect the urinary system and filtration processes of the kidneys. Librans are prone to urinary infections. Times of stress can also bring out skin problems such as eczema.

A gentle exercise regime will work wonders for Libra, as will a not too competitive sport. Playing tennis or golf are excellent activities for Librans. So too are dancercise sessions, yoga, and T'ai chi.

FAMOUS LIBRA PEOPLE

Oscar Wilde
Writer born October 16, 1854

Le Corbusier
Architect born October 6, 1887

John Lennon
Musician born October 9, 1940

Catherine Deneuve
French actress born October 22, 1943

Bob Geldof
Singer and political activist born October 5, 1951

Kate Winslet
British actress born October 5, 1975

Oscar Wilde

Life Mantra for Libra:

By creating my own happiness, I will find my well-being

Yoga will successfully de-stress a Libran

SCORPIO

The celestial Scorpion is a large constellation near the center of the Milky Way, its mighty tail curling through the night sky. In mythology, it is the creature sent to attack Orion. People of this sign have the stealth and steely determination of the Scorpion.

SCORPIO BASICS

This is the sign of power. Quiet and self-controlled, Scorpio people carry around them an aura of intensity. Not surprising, really, when you consider that Pluto—distant, icy, and dense—governs the sign. Astrologically, Scorpio is associated with extremes; potent, subtle, stealthy, and, like the Scorpion that represents this sign, sometimes deadly too. It may sound like heavy symbolism to describe a sign in this way, but it aptly conveys the gravitas carried by all those born under the sway of the Scorpion.

Scorpio belongs to the Fixed group of signs *(see page 10)*, which adds determination, persistence, and stubbornness to an individual's nature. Once Scorpio sets its mind on an objective, it focuses in until reaching its goal. Put all that together and you can see why Scorpio is so masterful.

Despite Scorpio's outward strength, purposefulness, and resilience, there is a deep, sensitive side to its character that only a few get to really see. This sign, after all, belongs to the Water element, which heightens the emotions. As with all Water-related signs, feelings rule Scorpio's life. Being the strong character that it is, means Scorpio's emotions are equally powerful. In fact, they can sometimes be overwhelmingly turbulent. No wonder, then, that Scorpios are known for their smoldering, passionate natures.

Of the 12 signs of the Zodiac, Scorpio is described as the most seductive. Magnetic, mysterious, and mesmeric: people can't help but be drawn to a compulsively charismatic personality in the same way that moths are drawn to a dangerous but compelling candle flame.

SCORPIO

Place in Zodiac Eighth
Birth Dates October 24–November 22
Symbol The Scorpion

Scorpio, from a series of reliefs depicting symbols and signs of the Zodiac, *c.* 1450, Rimini, Italy

WHAT MAKES SCORPIO HAPPY?

- Having a good spruce up
- Reading a gripping thriller
- Beating their opponent at chess
- A bathroom tiled in black
- Researching their family history
- Receiving a tax rebate
- A secluded cave
- A roller coaster ride
- Uncovering a mystery
- Stashing money away
- Sexy lingerie

YOUNG SCORPIOS

Young Scorpios are serious little children. Some say they are born old and wise. They like to make out they're tough. They may laugh back when they're teased; they may pretend it doesn't affect

SIGN ASSOCIATIONS

ZODIAC ESSENTIALS

Yin-Yang Yin
Element Water
Quality Fixed
Ruling Planet Pluto

OTHER AFFINITIES

Body Parts Groin, reproductive system, pelvis, organs of elimination, prostate gland
Color Claret red
Country Morocco
Flower Geranium
Gemstone Opal
Metal Steel
Tree Blackthorn
Weekday Tuesday

them when people call them names; they may show no pain when they fall and hurt themselves. Actually, it's all an act to protect their true feelings. Underneath, little Scorpios are very sensitive creatures who just want to be understood and loved. These children mature early and show great promise in scientific or technological studies. Both at school and university, they excel in subjects when left alone to do their own research. Socially, they tend to be fairly self-contained, but the true friends they make, they keep for life.

The Scorpio child has a natural interest in and aptitude for the sciences

SCORPIO'S BLIND SPOT

Harboring grudges is a bad habit of Scorpio

Never mess with a Scorpio! Not only are they the most jealous, possessive, controlling, intimidating, and menacing people on the planet, but there is something positively subterranean in the way they go about things—especially when it comes to getting their own back on people who have crossed them. They can wait years and years, scheming and plotting their revenge. Others will have long forgotten the transgression, but Scorpio never does. He or she will continue to harbor the slight until seeing an opportunity. Then, like the Scorpion with the sting poised, they seize their moment and—strike!

SCORPIO AS A PARENT

Because Scorpios are arch-inquisitors with a probing nature that is second-to-none, not a lot gets past the mothers and fathers of this sign. Call it intuition or simply downright suspicion, they somehow know what's going on. To their children, they are very encouraging and deeply caring, although a little overprotective at times. They can be strict—a hard stare from a Scorpio dad often suffices to keep discipline! Family loyalty for these parents is paramount. They will defend their brood against all onslaughts. Equally, they expect members to be true to their clan.

The female Scorpio is sensuously seductive in her favorite color

When it comes to relationships and romance, Scorpios believe all is fair in love and war. Unrelenting, when they set eyes on the object of their affection, they will not rest until they have conquered and won that heart. In all relationships, jealousy is a big problem. They can literally make themselves ill in the early stages of a partnership wondering where their partner is or who he or she may be with. However, they take their commitments, responsibilities, and vows seriously. To the one the Scorpion loves, he or she will remain devoted and faithful for life.

LOVE AND RELATIONSHIPS

Scorpios are essentially private people, and they usually keep their feelings to themselves. Their ruler Pluto, dark and mysterious, endows them with a certain enigmatic mystique.

Scorpios are not social mixers and do not especially enjoy small talk. They are selective about friendships, allowing only a few trusted people into their intimate circle. Those they do befriend, however, win lifelong loyalty and respect. Despite coming across as loners, Scorpios are not born to be alone. Fortunately, they are not short of admirers, because Scorpio has the reputation of being the sexiest sign in the Zodiac. Male Scorpios have smoldering good looks while their female counterparts are sensuously seductive.

PARTNERS IN LOVE

Passionate lovers, Scorpio people will give themselves completely to their partners, but jealousy can be a problem. These cosmic combinations reveal what might be expected from their relationships.

Scorpio with:

♈	**Aries**	Competitive drives ♥♥♥
♉	**Taurus**	Worth persisting ♥♥♥
♊	**Gemini**	Problematic ♥
♋	**Cancer**	Paradise ♥♥♥♥♥
♌	**Leo**	Differences ♥♥♥
♍	**Virgo**	Caring and sharing ♥♥♥♥
♎	**Libra**	Hard work ♥♥
♏	**Scorpio**	Soul connection ♥♥♥♥♥
♐	**Sagittarius**	Too distant ♥♥
♑	**Capricorn**	Good match ♥♥♥♥
♒	**Aquarius**	Rocky road ♥♥
♓	**Pisces**	Deeply loving ♥♥♥♥♥

Key: ♥ why bother? ♥♥ whenever ♥♥♥ wow ♥♥♥♥ wonderful ♥♥♥♥♥ well hot!

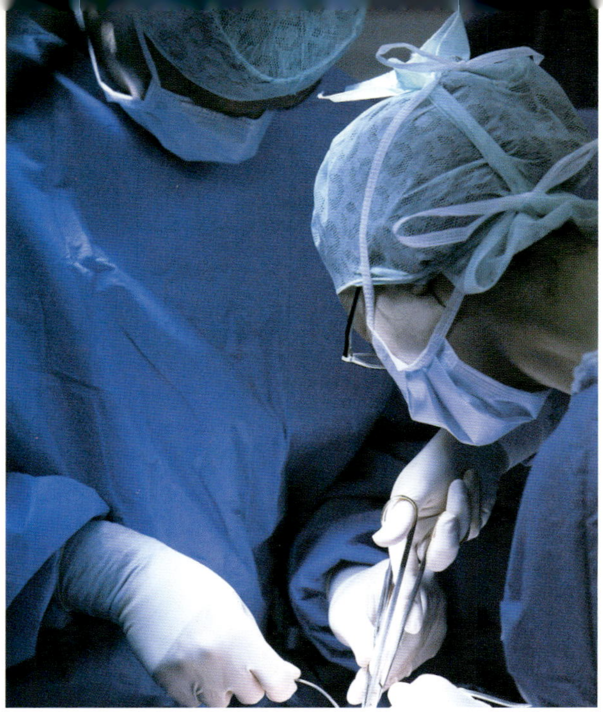

The field of surgery will fulfill Scorpionic ambitions

Life Mantra for Scorpio:

By expressing my feelings, I unlock my soul and connect with others

SCORPIO CAREER

The Scorpion is driven by curiosity. Little motivates it more than the desire to uncover a mystery, to delve, and discover the unknown. That's probably why Scorpios are so fascinated by all forms of research. Working in a laboratory, compiling data, or tracing family history keeps members of this sign happily occupied. The police service and all manner of detective work draw both Scorpio males and females. The world of finance is another area of interest since the sign governs insurance matters, taxes, loans, legacies, and escrow. Interestingly, it is also the sign of the occult, of surgery, sex, death, and the murky goings-on of the underworld.

Happy to toil away on their own on complex and confidential matters, Scorpios can work long hours and withstand a lot of pressure in order to crack it, to win through, and succeed. They live by a code of loyalty and, given a position of trust, will work faithfully for their employers. However, because all Scorpios have a tendency to control, they are perhaps more suited to running their own business. Ultimately, they succeed in business by following their intuition.

SUITABLE CAREERS

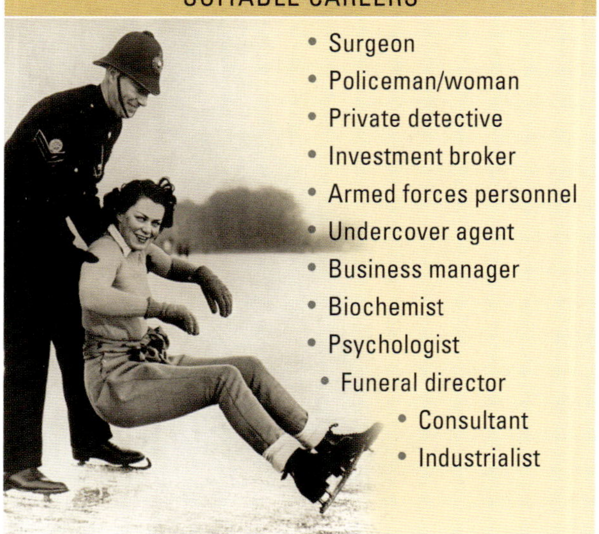

- Surgeon
- Policeman/woman
- Private detective
- Investment broker
- Armed forces personnel
- Undercover agent
- Business manager
- Biochemist
- Psychologist
- Funeral director
- Consultant
- Industrialist

MONEY MANAGEMENT

Scorpio is very savvy with money, and wealth equates with power for this sign. Scorpio people know how to earn it but, more importantly, they also know how to make money grow. In fact, because Scorpio is the sign of high finance and big business, they can be geniuses at handling cash affairs. Just as they are private about their emotions, so they also like to manage their money secretly, stashing some here, investing some there, tucking it into accounts that only they know about. Their income may come from a variety of sources or from a collection of portfolios. Or else, as many Scorpios do, they may gain from windfalls, successful investments, or from the generosity of other people.

Scorpio people are drawn to combative sports such as karate

BODY & HEALTH

Thankfully, Scorpios have strong constitutions, because they detest being ill. They believe in mind over matter, which seems to work for them. They are fairly active and take well to sports, especially combative ones such as karate or kickboxing. Or else they pit themselves against the elements as in mountaineering or long-distance running.

Participating in these extreme sports can trigger ruptures or hernias—conditions that are typically Scorpionic. Other health issues involve the reproductive system, including prostate problems and menstrual irregularities. So, too, are ailments connected with the excretory organs such as constipation or hemorrhoids.

On a more general basis, it is pent-up tension that tends to affect natives of this sign. A few tension release exercises night and morning can work wonders for the overwrought Scorpion.

FAMOUS SCORPIO PEOPLE

Pablo Picasso
Artist born October 25, 1881

Indira Gandhi
Indian leader born November 19, 1917

Grace Kelly
Actress born November 12, 1929

Bill Gates
Entrepreneur born October 28, 1955

Paul McKenna
Hypnotist born November 8, 1963

Julia Roberts
Actress born October 28, 1967

Pablo Picasso

SAGITTARIUS

Sagittarius, half-human and half-horse, is the centaur of mythology, the learned healer who forms a bridge between human beings and beasts. Also known as the Archer, Sagittarius is represented by the symbol of an arrow.

SAGITTARIUS BASICS

Just as the celestial Archer draws its bow and shoots arrows into the heavens, so the Sagittarian looks to the skies and shoots his or her ideas into the distance, often hitting the target full on.

Zodiac signs are grouped into Elements, and Qualities—a way of describing someone's character in a capsule *(see page 10)*. Sagittarius belongs to the groups of Fire and Mutability, and this makes for passionate, impulsive individuals who are able to bend and bow according to the situation or the company they are with. Open and friendly, a Sagittarian comes across as an easy-going person with a genial, expansive character.

SAGITTARIUS

Place in Zodiac Ninth
Birth Dates November 23–December 21
Symbol Archer/Centaur

***Archer with Red Bow*, painted by Georges Barbier in 1914**

People of this sign are popular among their peers. Socially outgoing, they are often quite the life-and-soul of the party.

Sagittarius has a huge appetite for life, a desire to travel and explore the world and experience all it has to offer, both physically and intellectually. No wonder this sign is known as the traveler of the Zodiac, never happier than when on the road or just roaming in the great outdoors.

Physically, Sagittarians need to keep active and thrive on sport—they are just as happy to compete individually as to join team games. Intellectually, the sign is associated with wisdom and philosophy. Life is the Sagittarian's university; a strong sense of reason and fair play are the marks of his or her integrity.

WHAT MAKES SAGITTARIUS HAPPY?

- Freedom
- Being in the great outdoors
- Jumping on a train, or plane or car and setting off into the sunset
- Thoughts of exotic places
- A herd of stallions galloping across the plain
- Home comforts
- A room piled floor to ceiling with books
- A loyal dog at their side
- A comfortable sweater
- A glass of wine at the end of the day

YOUNG ARCHERS

Young Sagittarians are happy, high-spirited souls who soon develop the strong independent side of their nature. Their innate curiosity, even from an early age, leads them to explore their environment, fearlessly climbing every obstacle as soon as they can crawl, just to see what's on the other side. As they grow, they are drawn to sports and enjoy all sorts of outdoor pursuits. The more academic children of this sign relish the chance to study and often excel in foreign languages.

SIGN ASSOCIATIONS

ZODIAC ESSENTIALS

Yin-Yang Yang

Element Fire

Quality Mutable

Ruling Planet Jupiter

OTHER AFFINITIES

Body Parts Thighs, liver, hepatic system, adipose fats

Color Royal purple

Country Australia

Flower Daisy

Gemstone Topaz

Metal Tin

Tree Oak

Weekday Thursday

Sagittarian fathers love to share stories with their children

SAGITTARIUS AS A PARENT

Sagittarian mothers and fathers encourage their youngsters to think for themselves from an early age. They use every opportunity to instruct and inform their children with stories and examples from their own experiences, as well as information they pick up. Physically active parents, they like to take their offspring hiking, camping, or farther afield to see the world, and they are always there on the sidelines cheering them on when playing their favorite sport.

SAGITTARIUS' BLIND SPOT

Over-the-top, much too friendly, cheerful, and enthusiastic? Yes, that describes Sagittarius well. But the Sagittarian should spare a thought for the quieter, more serious people among us who, for one reason or another, are unable to share in the exuberance. While Sagittarians are so passionate about their own religious or political point of view, they can sometimes fail to take into account that other people may have different, but just as valid, ideologies. They also suffer from foot-in-mouth syndrome – but they probably know all about that one by now!

LOVE AND RELATIONSHIPS

The casual, laid-back manner of Sagittarians, their beaming smile, and warm, friendly approach draw people to them like magnets. Before they know it, others are telling their life stories, often in the most intimate detail. So comfortable are Sagittarians to be with, that, even after knowing someone for 20 minutes, it feels like they've made a lifelong friend. Open and honest, frank, and forthright: what you see with a Sagittarian is what you get! What is also compelling

Friendly and often flirtatious behavior is normal for Sagittarians

about Sagittarians is that they are a fascinating mixture: fiercely independent on the one hand, while on the other they are among the most gregarious people in the Zodiac.

Sometimes a Sagittarian needs his or her own space—time to contemplate, commune with nature, and restore faith. At other times, he or she is the boisterous party animal, telling risqué jokes, and flirting like crazy. These two conflicting sides can have an impact on personal relationships and love life.

That self-reliance can make Sagittarians restless if they feel too hemmed in. It also means they are not in a hurry to hook into an intimate one-to-one. No wonder, then, that Sagittarius is known as the "sign of the Bachelor."

Then, just when it's least expected, Sagittarius will meet a soul-mate and fall head-over-heels in love. With the right partner—who knows when to cut enough slack and when to be loving—the Sagittarian will not only live happily ever after but also become a respected pillar of society.

PARTNERS IN LOVE

How does Sagittarius get on with the other signs of the Zodiac? Of course, everyone is unique, and you and your partner may be the exception to the rule. But, generally speaking, when it comes to love and relationships, astrology has some clear guidelines about who is a lover and who is a loser for the Archer.

Sagittarius with:

♈	**Aries**	You two just sizzle with passion! ♥♥♥♥♥
♉	**Taurus**	A difficult pairing ♥
♊	**Gemini**	Lots in common ♥♥♥
♋	**Cancer**	Short-term love ♥♥
♌	**Leo**	Capture this heart and never let it go! ♥♥♥♥♥
♍	**Virgo**	Your philosophies don't match ♥
♎	**Libra**	Fascinating combination ♥♥♥♥
♏	**Scorpio**	You can't take each other seriously ♥♥
♐	**Sagittarius**	A wonderful lifelong adventure ♥♥♥♥♥
♑	**Capricorn**	Oh dear, you irritate each other! ♥
♒	**Aquarius**	You bring out the best in each other ♥♥♥♥
♓	**Pisces**	Good companions, but that's all! ♥♥

Key: ♥ why bother? ♥♥ whenever ♥♥♥ wow ♥♥♥♥ wonderful ♥♥♥♥♥ well hot!

SAGITTARIAN CAREER

Whether working for themselves, as employers, or employees, Sagittarians have a reputation for being scrupulously fair. There isn't anything they would ask a colleague or underling to do that they wouldn't first do themselves. That's what earns them respect. This sign rules religion, higher education, publishing, medicine, and the law—all vocations and professions to which Sagittarians are drawn. This is also the sign of foreign affairs, travel, tourism, and faraway places, and Sagittarians are often found in occupations encompassing these lines of business.

In work as in life, if you're a Sagittarian, you believe in honesty and are always prepared to give others a chance to speak their minds—right or wrong. Like all Fire signs, Sagittarians enjoy their fair share of flattery. However, because they

Life Mantra for Sagittarius:

The world is a beautiful place that fills my soul with wonderment and joy

SUITABLE CAREERS

- Sportsman or Woman
- Travel agent
- Lecturer
- Lawyer
- Broadcaster
- Editor
- Physician
- Judge
- Translator
- Member of the clergy

Casual, informal, and sporty—that's the image of Sagittarius

are blessed with exquisite insight, they know a bluff when they see one, and are able quickly to despatch anyone they believe is taking them for a ride. They also know a good opportunity when they come across it, and fate sends more than the average lucky chances their way.

MONEY MANAGEMENT

Sagittarians are fortunate to be born as they are because this is the luckiest sign in the Zodiac. Being both lucky and philosophical means that these people tend not to be too financially bothered when young. Money seems to come when they need it at that age, and if it doesn't, well—they tighten the belt and think of higher things. It's when a Sagittarian reaches middle age that he or she starts to become financially savvy and acquire a true money sense. Whether by accident or design, these people seem able to hit a rich seam, or to be in the right place at just the right time. Although there is always the exception, astrologers say it is unusual to find an impecunious member of this sign.

BODY & HEALTH

Sagittarian men simply don't look comfortable in a collar and tie. Women belonging to this sign do wear stilettos, pencil skirts, and chic ensembles like the rest of their Zodiacal sisters. But to tell the truth, they're not only happier, but also far sexier, in sweaters and jeans, with their hair tousled, and a fresh bloom to their cheeks.

If you are a member of the Sagittarian tribe, you will know only too well how easily you put on weight, especially on your hips, buttocks, and thighs. Want to stay in trim? Think about the emblem of the sign: half-horse, half-human! Sagittarius was designed to run and gallop and roam. So for Sagittarius, staying fit and keeping those inches off means getting out into the fresh air, hiking, jogging, and skating—or, alternatively, joining the local baseball or basketball team. Staying active keeps a Sagittarian happy, healthy, and in shape.

An ambitious Sagittarian can forge a successful career in medicine

FAMOUS SAGITTARIUS PEOPLE

Ludwig van Beethoven
Composer born
December 16, 1770

Winston Churchill
British Prime Minister born
November 30, 1874

Tina Turner
Singer born
November 26, 1938

Jimi Hendrix
Musician born
November 27, 1942

Kim Basinger
Actress born December 8, 1953

Brad Pitt
Actor born December 18, 1963

Jimi Hendrix

SAGITTARIUS

♑ CAPRICORN

The smallest constellation of the Zodiac, Capricorn is named from the Latin for "goat horn" and is known as the sea-goat because of its location in an area of the heavens called the Sea. It is linked with the Babylonian god Ea and Greek demigod Pan.

CAPRICORN BASICS

Capricorn is the sign of ambition. Cardinal in quality and belonging to the Earth element *(see page 10)* gives its natives a practical, no-nonsense disposition. If you were born into this group, you know how robust and resilient you are. The Earth element ensures you keep your feet on the ground while the Cardinal drive propels you into motion. No wonder you are so industrious, always on the go—reaching, striving, working, turning ideas into reality.

Capricorn is ruled by Saturn, planet of discipline and structure. Saturn is known as the great taskmaster of the universe. It is a stern energy that teaches us how to work within limitations and to make the best out of difficult situations. Saturn hones and refines. It urges us to set goals, work hard, and ever keep our eye on that objective in the distance—success.

Indeed, to achieve success, status, position, affluence, and wealth are the ultimate aim for every Capricorn. Getting there may at times feel like climbing a mountain. But no matter how steep or precipitous the path, like the goat that represents the sign, Capricorn will slowly and cautiously make its way up until it reaches the very top. Stoicism is a key characteristic. Of all the signs, Capricorn is the most dutiful. Members of the sign were born to take on responsibility and with a passive acceptance bear burdens that would simply floor other people. What helps to lighten the load is their wry take on life. They are witty, with a wonderfully dry sense of humor that often has their friends creased with laughter.

CAPRICORN

Place in Zodiac Tenth
Birth Dates December 22–January 20
Symbol The Goat

WHAT MAKES CAPRICORN HAPPY?

- Being a member of the trendiest club in town
- Winning an election
- Designer shoes, shirts, and bags
- A personal invitation to a society wedding
- A box at the opera
- A case of fine wine
- Bringing home the blue rosette from "best dog in show"
- Being chauffeur-driven to work

YOUNG CAPRICORNS

Because they are painfully shy, Capricorn children tend to be solitary souls. It takes time for them to get accustomed to new faces and places. Making new friends can be an agony. Not until well past their teenage years do these youngsters develop the confidence to socialize and be at ease in the

Italian Baroque painting of Pan, the faun-like demigod who is linked with Capricorn in Greek mythology

SIGN ASSOCIATIONS

ZODIAC ESSENTIALS

Element Earth
Quality Cardinal
Ruling Planet Saturn

OTHER AFFINITIES

Body Parts Skin, teeth, hair, bones, knees, elbows
Color Forest green
Country India
Flower Pansy
Gemstone Garnet
Metal Lead
Tree Yew
Weekday Saturday

CAPRICORN'S BLIND SPOT

A Capricorn can be a real wet blanket. Miserable, miserly, strict, and stern, people belonging to this sign can be party poopers par excellence. They are cynical and demoralizing, judgmental and controlling, always believing they know best and expecting those around them to do what they are told. These people are dour. They can spread doom and gloom even among the happiest of crowds. What's more, if their efforts aren't justly rewarded, or if they fail to achieve their goals, they can turn sour and resentful. Snobbish, mean-minded, and unforgiving, they look down on anyone they consider inferior and look up enviously at anyone who has more than they do.

company of others. Born with old heads on young shoulders, Capricorn children work diligently and study hard to achieve good grades. They strive to win merit badges and are in their element when given class honors or made a prefect. Obedient, sensible, and responsible, these youngsters tend to be well-behaved, considerate, and polite. They mature early and respond best when treated like young adults. At school and university they are drawn to practical subjects, earth sciences, business studies, math, and technology.

CAPRICORN AS A PARENT

The future well-being of their children is uppermost in the mind of every Capricorn mother and father. These parents expect their children to work hard and to achieve things. They will not tolerate rebellion, laziness, or untidiness. They can be quite stingy financially, believing

The Capricorn student works hard and is a high achiever in subjects such as math and business studies

Capricorns tend to form their long-term relationships at work

that to be a good example for teaching prudence. They care deeply for their children but may not be overtly affectionate. Capricorns often put their work first and consequently can miss out on a lot of family fun.

LOVE AND RELATIONSHIPS

Whether it is because people born under the sign of the Goat are shy, or because they usually put work before fun, or even because they are selective over the crowd they mix with, the upshot is that Capricorns tend to come across as starchy and aloof. For whatever reason, Capricorns in general don't make friends easily. When young, they are drawn more to the company of older people. Later, they gravitate into professional circles, often mixing business with pleasure or striking acquaintances with people of influence and power. As a consequence, members of the sign form their main long-term friendships with people at work. Their romantic liaisons are often with a colleague, workmate, or boss.

Capricorns are arguably the most aspirational people in the universe. Being realists, they know that love on a shoestring isn't enough to sustain a relationship. So, when looking for a mate, they set their sights on someone who is well-heeled or well-connected, or otherwise a partner who is prepared to work hard and help them attain prosperity.

Capricorns are not frivolous creatures. They are serious and dislike playing games, especially not psychological or emotional ones. In matters of the heart, they take commitments and vows seriously, and believe in fidelity.

PARTNERS IN LOVE

When it comes to love, Capricorn deals straight and fair. Emotional blackmailing is out, but to the partner who matches Capricorn's high standards of excellence, the Goat will remain true for life.

Capricorn with:

♈	**Aries**	Rewarding in many ways ♥♥♥
♉	**Taurus**	A match made in heaven ♥♥♥♥♥
♊	**Gemini**	Different desires ♥♥
♋	**Cancer**	Opposites but very supportive ♥♥♥♥
♌	**Leo**	Discordant ♥♥
♍	**Virgo**	Made to last a lifetime ♥♥♥♥♥
♎	**Libra**	Limited prospects ♥♥
♏	**Scorpio**	Well suited ♥♥♥♥
♐	**Sagittarius**	Out of tune ♥
♑	**Capricorn**	Powerfully motivated ♥♥♥♥♥
♒	**Aquarius**	An awkward match ♥♥
♓	**Pisces**	Quite entrancing ♥♥♥♥

Key: ♥ why bother? ♥♥ whenever ♥♥♥ wow ♥♥♥♥ wonderful ♥♥♥♥♥ well hot!

Architecture is a good field of industry for Capricorn

Life Mantra for Capricorn:

Through trust I relinquish control and find my heart's ease

CAPRICORNIAN CAREER

The genius of Capricorn is to create order out of chaos. That is what makes Capricorn people such brilliant organizers. That, and the fact that they are prepared to work constantly to get the results they want. They are ambitious—prosperity and wealth are their ultimate goals in life. So they will skimp and scrape for that designer suit to look the part at work, for the executive car to make a good impression, and for the house with the prestigious address. Once they have a foot on a rung of the corporate ladder, it's only a matter of time before they make their way right up to the top. Few could fault Capricorn's industriousness, conscientious approach, and ability to shoulder responsibility.

SUITABLE CAREERS

- Administrator
- Estate agent
- Politician
- Manager
- Organizer
- Chief executive
- Architect
- Town planner
- Civil servant
- Surveyor
- Government official
- Engineer

As employees, they give of their best at all times. As employers, they are workaholics. Steady, sober, and conservative in their ways, they also have a ruthless streak and won't tolerate poor workmanship.

MONEY MANAGEMENT

Capricorn knows how to be economical. Saturn, the sign's ruler, is the planet of restriction, an austere energy that teaches the value of saving and the perils of waste. Capricorns can tighten their belts and go without as long as they know that their sacrifice today will lead to a better, more prosperous tomorrow. They love the fine things that money can buy, but are not prepared to take risks with their hard-earned cash. Careful and steady, they hoard every cent and stash it away in the savings bank, or even in a box under the bed. Typically, if they invest, it will be with blue-chip companies, solid and secure. Knowing that the money is safe and that they are quietly amassing a tidy nest egg lets them sleep well at night.

Hoarding money suits the spirit of Capricorn

BODY & HEALTH

Want to hear the good news, Capricorn? Members of your sign seem to have discovered the secret of longevity. After all, the ruling planet, Saturn, is known as the Father of Time, and it is said there are more octo- and nonagenarians among this astrological group than any other in the Zodiac. Want to know even better news? The older a Capricorn grows, the younger he or she seems to look.

Now for the down side. Skin, teeth, bones, knees—these are Capricorn's weak links, which can give trouble throughout life. Capricorns are prone to conditions such as acne, eczema, and shingles, especially when they go through periods of stress. Drinking plenty of water can help to keep the complexion clear.

A Capricorn's knees need extra protection. Avoid high-impact exercises that put pressure on your joints. Instead, take up golf, walk, cycle, or practice Pilates. Because the skeleton in general is ruled by Capricorn, members of this sign can be predisposed to degenerative diseases of the joints and bones such as rheumatism and osteoporosis.

FAMOUS CAPRICORN PEOPLE

Chairman Mao
Chinese leader born December 26, 1893

Al Capone
Gangster born January 17, 1899

Richard Nixon
President born January 9, 1913

Ava Gardner
Actress born December 24, 1922

Martin Luther King, Jr.
Civil Rights activist born January 15, 1929

Muhammad Ali
Boxer born January 17, 1942

Kate Moss
Model born January 16, 1974

Muhammad Ali

AQUARIUS

The third of the Air signs, Aquarius is linked with Ganymede, the youthful cupbearer of the gods, among other legendary figures. The sign is known as the "water carrier" and represented by a human figure pouring water from a jug.

AQUARIUS BASICS

Despite the watery connections, Aquarius actually belongs to the Air element. This means that, like Gemini and Libra, the other Air signs, Aquarius is mentally alert, open, friendly, and curious about anything and everything that is new.

The Air element encompasses a wide range of concepts that apply to the sign. On the one hand, it is associated with speech and communications. Talking "hot air," "gassing," "shooting the breeze," these are the "airy" metaphors we use to describe the way we verbally express ourselves. Certainly, Aquarians relish a good debate and long chats with their friends. They have strong points of view about politics and they won't hesitate to give their opinion about how to sort out society's ills. This element is also linked to the intellect, the workings of the mind, and the power of ideas. In fact, Aquarius is the visionary of the Zodiac. Aquarian people are able to key into advanced concepts, see links, and connections that are invisible to other eyes, to understand motivations, unravel emotions, and foresee cycles, and trends far into the distant future.

Aquarius is an extraordinary mixture, living in today but thinking in tomorrow's world. It is precisely because Aquarians are able to take in the wider scheme of things that they don't feel bound to live within present-day customs and mores. Seeing beyond society's current norms and moralities essentially makes them unconventional, a little eccentric perhaps, but fundamentally unique and free spirits.

AQUARIUS

Place in Zodiac Eleventh
Birth Dates January 21–February 19
Symbol The Water-Bearer

WHAT MAKES AQUARIUS HAPPY?

- Meeting new people
- Giving advice to others
- Flying an airplane
- Mastering new machines
- New Age paraphernalia and horoscopes
- Hosting a conference
- Winning at Canasta
- Doing whacky things to raise money for charity
- Stargazing at midnight
- Sci-fi stories

YOUNG AQUARIANS

From the word go, Aquarian children show a burning curiosity about their world. Even before they learn to talk they will use all their senses to explore the environment around them, turning objects this way and that, working out how things function and fit together. Once they discover language, they don't stop asking questions.

A portrait of Aquarius by the 17th-century Flemish painter Jacob Jordaens

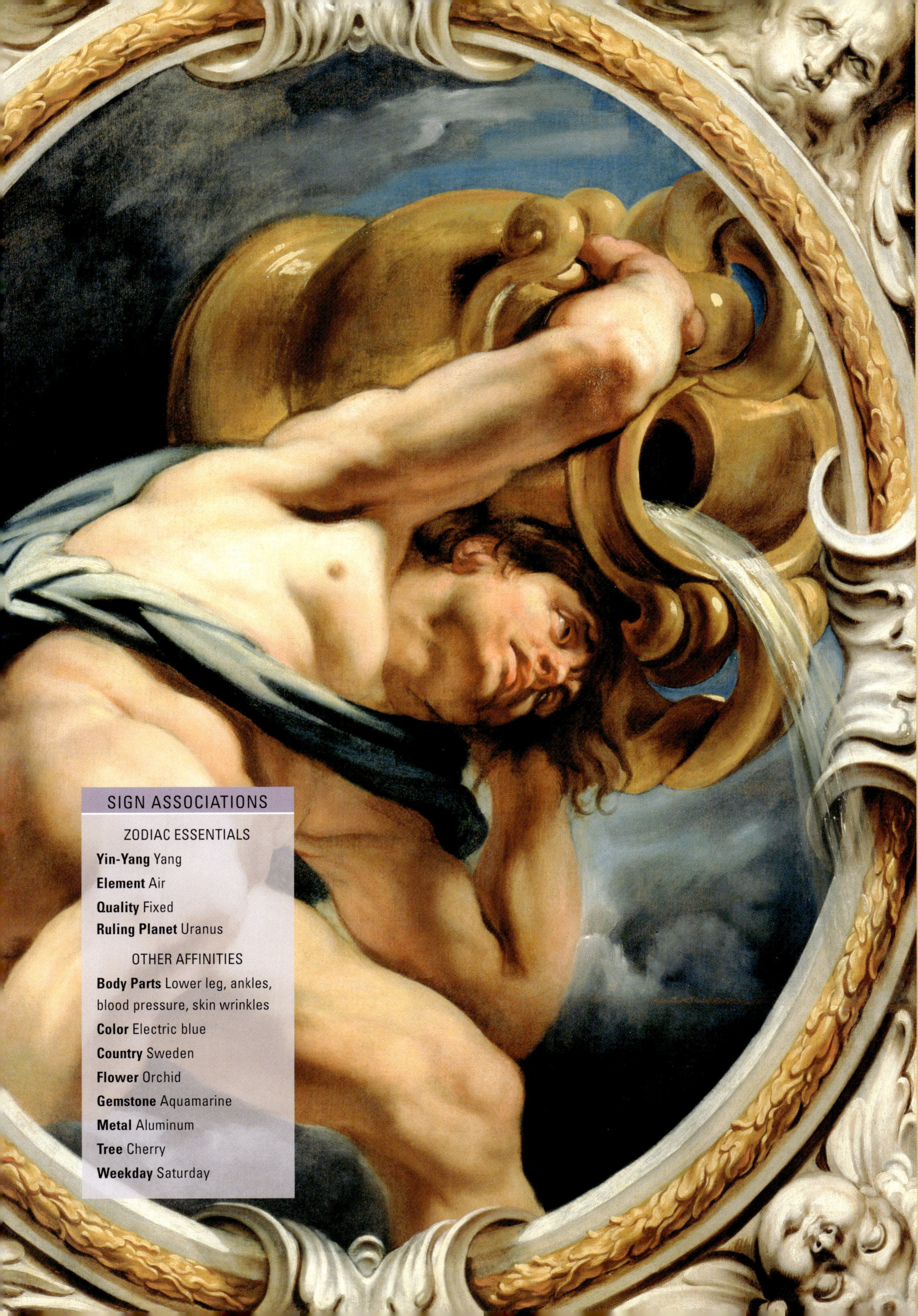

SIGN ASSOCIATIONS

ZODIAC ESSENTIALS

Yin-Yang Yang
Element Air
Quality Fixed
Ruling Planet Uranus

OTHER AFFINITIES

Body Parts Lower leg, ankles, blood pressure, skin wrinkles
Color Electric blue
Country Sweden
Flower Orchid
Gemstone Aquamarine
Metal Aluminum
Tree Cherry
Weekday Saturday

AQUARIUS' BLIND SPOT

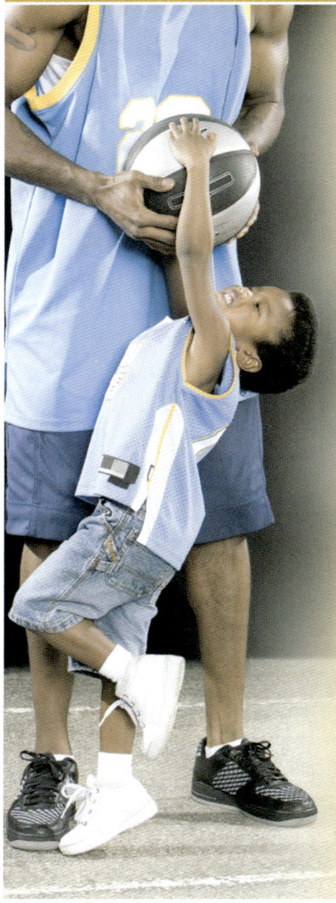

Aquarians can be thoroughly contrary. They are unpredictable and, quite simply, perverse. Go with the flow? Never! Tell them to do one thing, and they'll very likely do the exact opposite. Opinionated, stubborn, and rebellious, they disregard rules, conventions and even the law if it suits them. Inflexible and dogmatic, an Aquarian can never believe or admit that he or she is wrong.

The Aquarian instinct is to be awkward in absolutely everything, which makes even playing a game with them difficult

Math, science, and computer technology are the subjects that fascinate these youngsters most. As they grow, they can become little rebels—they are, after all, ruled by Uranus, planet of revolution! Sociable and laidback, they dislike formality and following rules in general. As they grow, they develop strong political ideas and are often found in the thick of student protests.

AQUARIUS AS A PARENT

Just as Aquarians are fascinated by observing structures and analyzing systems, so they are enchanted by the whole process of parenthood. To them, rearing children is like watching an experiment come together. They delight in teaching their children, reading stories, and explaining how the world works. Tolerant and relaxed, they give their offspring a liberal upbringing and encourage independence from an early age.

LOVE AND RELATIONSHIPS

It is not surprising that an Aquarian is such a gregarious individual. After all, the sign governs friends, associations, groups, and societies. Aquarians are drawn to people, relaxed in the company of others, and they enjoy mixing with a wide and varied crowd. It gives them pleasure to analyze human feelings and behavior, although they themselves are not driven by emotions. Rather, they take a cool, intellectual approach to matters of the heart.

Male Aquarians are disarmingly charming, while their female counterparts are glamorous and vivacious—so they have little trouble

Aquarians are strongly motivated to join in with student protests and public demonstrations

attracting potential mates. However, they prize their personal freedom and need a partner who will understand their need to do their own thing, unfettered, without having to constantly explain. Aquarians are drawn to intelligent, independent people with whom they can share intellectual conversations and pursuits.

In love, Aquarians are immensely tender and caring, although perhaps not overly physically demonstrative. Essentially democratic, they value a partnership based on equality. Their home life may hint at the Bohemian with informal customs and relaxed domestic rules. However, because friendships form an integral part of their personal life, an Aquarian's house will always be a magnet to friends and visitors of all kinds.

Aquarians are charming and vivacious

PARTNERS IN LOVE

Aquarian relationships are likely to reflect their unconventional beliefs. Many form unusual partnerships, settling down happily in open marriages, for example. This is how they fit with other signs.

Aquarius with:

♈	**Aries**	Intriguing delights ♥♥♥♥
♉	**Taurus**	A stubborn pair! ♥♥
♊	**Gemini**	Unstoppable ♥♥♥♥♥
♋	**Cancer**	Two very different people ♥♥
♌	**Leo**	Highly volatile ♥♥
♍	**Virgo**	Boring ♥♥
♎	**Libra**	Absolutely wonderful ♥♥♥♥♥
♏	**Scorpio**	Needs insight ♥♥
♐	**Sagittarius**	Long-lasting love ♥♥♥♥
♑	**Capricorn**	Heavy going ♥♥
♒	**Aquarius**	Shared passions ♥♥♥♥♥
♓	**Pisces**	Flighty fun ♥♥♥

Key: ♥ why bother? ♥♥ whenever ♥♥♥ wow ♥♥♥♥ wonderful ♥♥♥♥♥ well hot!

AQUARIAN CAREER

Aquarius is known as the sign of genius. Being ruled both by Air, the element of the intellect, and by Uranus, the Great Awakener, gives natives of this sign an original and inspirational turn of mind. In short, this is the sign most associated with inventors and pioneers. Drawn to mechanical, electrical, or hi-tech equipment, they're whizz-kids with machinery, computers, and gadgetry of all kinds. They can always see how to improve a system.

Aquarians are good reformers, too: humanitarian at heart, strongly community-minded, and with a social conscience that drives them into jobs that either provide a service or that help humankind. Democracy is fundamental to the Aquarian mind. Whether as an employee or director of the company, they believe in equality, and that everyone should have a say. Even so, they like to do things their own way—after all, this is a Fixed sign, which means they can be rigid in their views. But there is also that rebellious streak in Aquarians that makes them kick against bureaucracy and despise red-tape.

Life Mantra for Aquarius:

I rejoice in my uniqueness of spirit and acknowledge that my strength lies in being an individual

The sign of Aquarius is associated with inventors and pioneers

SUITABLE CAREERS

- Councillor
- Electrician
- Engineer
- Astrologer
- Inventor
- Airline personnel
- Mechanic
- Sociologist
- Adviser
- Consultant
- Politician
- Analyst
- Economist
- Manufacturer
- Technician

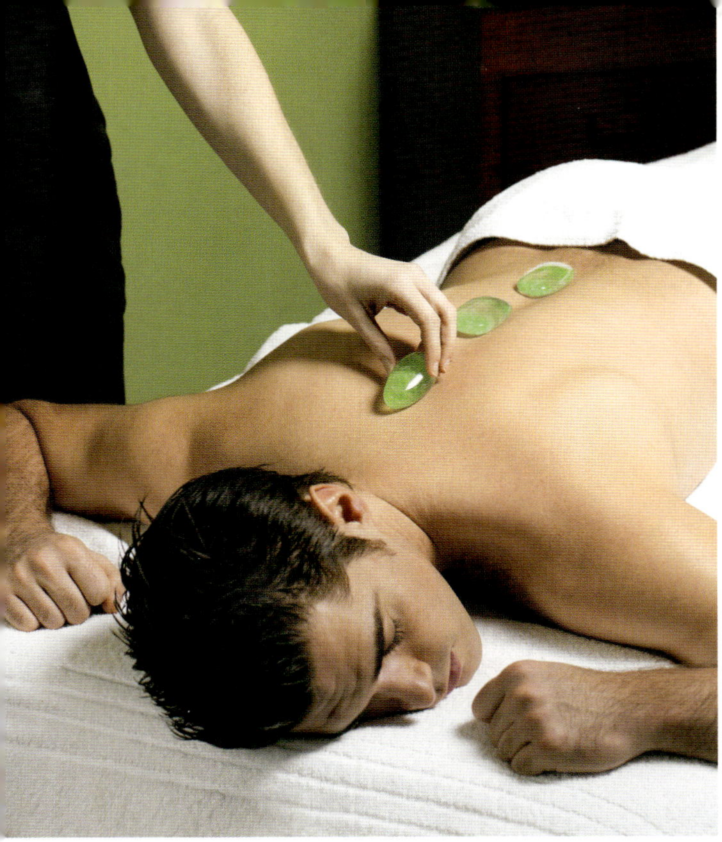

Alternative medicine especially appeals to Aquarius

BODY & HEALTH

Aquarius is generally sound of health. So long as these people don't feel hemmed in physically, psychologically, or emotionally, they jog along nicely through life. If problems do happen, they tend to occur suddenly, in the form of unusual injuries or accidents—again, this comes from the rulership of Uranus. However, Uranus is also associated with experimentation, and Aquarians are especially drawn to trying out different techniques, alternative medicine, or complementary therapies.

The lower leg, specifically from the knee to the ankle, is ruled by Aquarius. Weaknesses here can manifest themselves in conditions such as varicose veins. More typically, however, Aquarians are prone to twisted ankles. The cardiovascular system is also associated with this sign, and high blood pressure is a problem affecting some Aquarians as they age. Regular exercise will help stave off hypertension and keep the Aquarian heart in good shape.

MONEY MANAGEMENT

Aquarians are not essentially money-oriented, nor are they driven to amass possessions as a sense of security or status symbol. Essentially, the Aquarian mind is on higher things. What money does buy the Aquarian, however, is space and time to do the things he or she wants, to pursue personal interests, and to experiment and explore.

Aquarians are not sentimental people, but they are idealists. Many are patrons and benefactors, putting their money into good causes. They do not actively pursue riches for the sake of it. Nevertheless they do make money, often through their inventions, by happenstance, or serendipitously. Such things in an Aquarian's life can be traced to the influence of Uranus.

FAMOUS AQUARIAN PEOPLE

Charles Darwin
Naturalist born February 12, 1809

Abraham Lincoln
President also born February 12, 1809

Jules Verne
French novelist born February 8, 1828

James Dean
Actor born February 8, 1931

Yoko Ono
Artist born February 18, 1933

Vanessa Redgrave
Actress born January 30, 1937

Oprah Winfrey
TV host born January 29, 1954

Vanessa Redgrave

♓ PISCES

From the Latin for "fish," Pisces is represented by two fish entwined by a long cord in the night sky. Belonging to the Water element, and ruled by Neptune, much about Pisces is fluid and flowing. It is the twelfth and last sign of the Zodiac.

PISCES BASICS

Like Gemini, which is symbolized by the Twins, Pisces also comprises a dual nature with its symbol of the Fish. The two fish are bound together but swimming in opposite directions. This is what makes Pisces such a complex sign and why its natives are so paradoxical. Neptune, planet of illusion, adds a further intangibility and mystique. Mysteries, fantasies, and dreams surround these individuals. Many are gifted artists, musicians, or writers who live in their imaginations.

There's an almost insubstantial quality to Pisces. Described as Mutable and belonging to the Water element further underscores the constantly changing nature of the Pisces individual—the emotions that are always in flux, the fluidity of thought, and the lack of structure is so common among members of this sign. Just like water that takes the shape of the vessel into which it is poured, Pisceans are so changeable that they are able to mold themselves into any role.

Pisceans are gentle and kind-hearted people who are often prepared to sublimate their own desires in order to make the lives of others happy and comfortable. They abhor arguments and, like fish who have an instinctive response to swim away from trouble, so Pisces folk will instantly withdraw from any difficult or unpleasant situation—if not physically, then mentally by retreating into a fantasy world they create for themselves.

PISCES

Place in Zodiac Twelfth
Birth Dates February 20–March 20
Symbol The Fish

WHAT MAKES PISCES HAPPY?

- Watching fluffy clouds scudding across an azure sky
- A season ticket to the theater
- Cathedral services
- A glass of mulled wine on a cold winter's night
- Sepia photographs from a bygone age
- Standing barefoot on freshly mown grass
- Finding a sanctuary
- Having a secret to keep and hold dear

YOUNG PISCEANS

Leave young Pisceans to their own devices and they will happily create for themselves a wonderful world of magical make-believe. Angelic little souls who melt the heart, these children need delicate nurturing. Their creative and dramatic abilities, such as writing wonderful stories and painting fabulous pictures, are innate skills that come to the fore from a very early age. On the flip-side, they have a tendency to daydream when

Detail of fresco in the Villa Medici in Florence, showing the symbolic Piscean fish placed upon the head of a female figure

SIGN ASSOCIATIONS

ZODIAC ESSENTIALS

Yin-Yang Yin
Element Water
Quality Mutable
Ruling Planet Neptune

OTHER AFFINITIES

Body Parts Feet, toes, mucous linings
Color Sea green
Country Portugal
Flower Sweet pea
Gemstone Bloodstone
Metal Platinum
Tree Willow
Weekday Thursday

PISCES' BLIND SPOT

Vague, weak-willed, evasive, and downright dishonest, Pisceans are fantasists of the first order. Their indecision, lack of moral fiber, and inability to think matters through causes confusion and difficulties for everyone around them. When things get tough, they simply walk away leaving other people to clear up the mess. They're emotionally clingy, pouring their beings into other people, and expecting to be carried. If things don't go their way, they instantly think they're being victimized and they sulk—for days. They may be pacifists but they know how to turn the screw and make others feel guilty for daring to upset them.

Pisces will walk away from a problem

lessons become boring or difficult. Socially, these youngsters are wary of other people and tend to have few friends. They avoid noisy, boisterous classmates and naturally gravitate toward those quieter, calmer companions with whom they feel easy and comfortable. The Humanities, Art, Drama, or Music schools beckon Pisceans as they move into adulthood.

PISCES AS A PARENT

Astrologically, Pisces is considered fecund and fertile. Many people of this sign either give birth to twins or have larger than average families. As parents, they are devoted to their brood. Gentle and caring, they adore reading stories to their youngsters and encourage their children to express their imagination in any way possible. Mothers and fathers born under this sign can be fairly relaxed when it comes to rules and regulations —often too lax and even somewhat slapdash

Piscean children are very creative and adore painting

Shy, with doe-like eyes, is Pisces

when it comes to giving parental guidance. Confrontations upset them, so they would rather give in to their children's demands than engage in an argument.

LOVE AND RELATIONSHIPS

There is something tantalizingly alluring about people born under Pisces. It could be their soft, kind manner or their doe-like, lustrous eyes that makes people rush to protect them. Shy one minute and sociable the next, they are confusing creatures—as much to themselves as they are to others.

PARTNERS IN LOVE

Driven both by their hearts and their imaginations, Pisceans are intrinsically impressionable and all too often fall for the most unsuitable mates. The worst and best matches can be seen here.

Pisces with:

♈	**Aries**	Challenging passion ♥
♉	**Taurus**	Mutual minds and hearts ♥♥♥♥
♊	**Gemini**	Probably chalk and cheese ♥
♋	**Cancer**	Deeply romantic ♥♥♥♥♥
♌	**Leo**	A tantalizing affair ♥♥♥
♍	**Virgo**	Hard work ♥♥
♎	**Libra**	A genteel liaison ♥♥♥
♏	**Scorpio**	Ardent and magnetic ♥♥♥♥♥
♐	**Sagittarius**	Emotionally distant ♥♥
♑	**Capricorn**	Mutually rewarding ♥♥♥♥
♒	**Aquarius**	Reasonable, but lacks understanding ♥♥
♓	**Pisces**	A good relationship ♥♥♥♥♥

Key: ♥ why bother? ♥♥ whenever ♥♥♥ wow ♥♥♥♥ wonderful ♥♥♥♥♥ bangin'

Ruled by Water, Pisceans are led by their emotions, intuitively following an inner voice that comes from deep within. What they're looking for is a love affair that sweeps them off their feet and transports them to a place where they can live happily ever after. What these people need is a soul-mate with whom to share life's rich adventures, to dream their dreams as one, and together forge a deep and lasting rapport.

Rarely is life that simple, however, for Pisces. For these gentle and loving folk are basically indecisive. In love, they will put their partners on a pedestal only to suffer devastating sadness and disillusionment if they discover the object of their affection has feet of clay.

Both male and female Pisces people make wonderful companions and will do anything for those they love. With the right partner who will ground, cherish, and adore them—and tend to the mundane necessities of daily life—they will be in heaven. The big challenge for Pisceans, though, is to maintain the impetus once the first flush of high romance has faded, else they may perpetually feel that life is a big disappointment.

The world of theater will attract a Piscean

SUITABLE CAREERS

- Pharmacist
- Photographer
- Nurse
- Fiction writer
- Podiatrist
- Shoe designer
- Charity worker
- Undercover agent
- Bartender
- Welfare worker
- Poet
- Warden
- Psychiatrist
- Actor
- Film director

PISCEAN CAREER

Pisces' strength lies in the power of imagination, so it isn't surprising to find that these people are drawn to occupations that are essentially creative. The world of the Arts is a special lure, either as artisan or commentator in this field. Pisceans are always drawn to the bright lights, to showbiz and the world of glamor. Dancing, singing, and acting are ideal career paths for these people who live for their fantasies.

Pisceans can work on their own quite happily in a studio or office, or freelance at home. Working in a big company can present problems, however, because these people do not function well under stress of any kind. Competitive situations can make them physically ill. In a calm atmosphere, with pleasant surroundings and engaged in a congenial line of work, their talents will flourish.

Life Mantra for Pisces:

By staying grounded and creating boundaries, I harness my talents in order to fulfill my dreams

Pisceans are compassionate people whose ability to empathize with the suffering of others often takes them into the healing professions. They make fine doctors, nurses, psychologists, and psychiatrists.

FAMOUS PISCES PEOPLE

Michelangelo
Artist born March 6, 1475

Victor Hugo
Poet born February 26, 1802

Albert Einstein
Physicist born March 14, 1879

John Steinbeck
Writer born February 27, 1902

Elizabeth Taylor
Actress born February 27, 1932

Michael Caine
Actor born March 14, 1933

Sharon Stone
Actress born March 10, 1958

Michael Caine

MONEY MANAGEMENT

Pisces is perhaps the least materialistic of all the Zodiac signs. People of this sign are not interested in money per se. If they have money in their pockets, they are likely to give it away to charity. Unfortunately, this means that they are not financially savvy. Worst of all, Pisceans are easy prey to anyone unscrupulous enough to play on their kindheartedness.

On the whole, Pisces folk are content to spend what they earn and because they tend to be dreamers, they often forget to save for that proverbial rainy day. But not all Pisceans end up paupers. Indeed, many amass considerable wealth through their creative talents. Finding themselves a good financial adviser who will show them how to invest their cash wisely is a must.

BODY & HEALTH

Pisceans are prone to problems with their feet. This can range from recurrent chilblains to troublesome bunions, and in extreme cases to gout. For Pisces people, ensuring they have good fitting shoes from the minute they learn to walk, and avoiding faddish fashions through their teens, should help to lessen potential problems later.

Apart from the physical health problems, Pisceans have a tendency to have depression. They are, in the main, hypersensitive and vulnerable individuals who quickly run low of energy and vitality. The greatest danger is when their dreams are shattered. That's when they withdraw into themselves, often seeking comfort in alcohol or other substances. Pisces is said to be the sign of addiction. However, these are remarkably resilient folk who, like the fish that represents this sign, will bob back to the surface. Every so often Pisces folk should get away from the hubbub of other people and find a sanctuary where they can re-charge their batteries—physically, emotionally, and spiritually.

INDEX

RECOMMENDED READING

Kempton-Smith, Debbi. *Secrets From A Stargazer's Notebook*: Topquark Press.
Parker, Derek and Julia. *Parkers' Astrology:* DK.
Parker, Derek and Julia. *Kiss Book Of Astrology*: DK.
Reid, Lori. *Love Signs*: Duncan Baird.
Reid, Lori. *Moon Magic*: Carlton Books.
Reid, Lori. *Sun & Moon Signs*: Duncan Baird.
Sakoian, Frances, and Acker, Louis. *The Astrologer's Handbook.*
West, Peter. *Astrology And Childhood*: London House.

Web sites to visit for astrological information or to have your birth chart drawn up: www.alabe.com, www.astrodient.com, www.astrodatabank.com.

ACKNOWLEDGMENTS

The publishers would like to thank the following for permission to reproduce copyright material:

AKG: center images on pp 24, 30, 36, 42, 48, 54, 60, 66, 72, 78, 84, 90.

ALAMY: pp 1, 2.

Blue Island: pp 12 (bottom left), 14 (bottom left), and all the astrological glyphs throughout book.

Getty Images: pp 25, 29 (bottom right), 31, 35, 36, 37, 67, 77, 84 (bottom), 85, 86, 87, 88, 89.

All other images are courtesy of Corbis.